On Being F.

What, Like It's I

To Hollie,

You are such a ray
of sun in both mine and
Louis's life! Never change!

I hope you enjoy my

little book,

With love

Alex ♡

Alexandra Walker-Jones

I dedicate this book to my parents, Rebecca, and Chris, for being a steadfast source of advice, exemplar, words of wisdom, and support to me for all of my life.

Table of Contents

Preface

I have struggled. Admittedly, not with finding happiness or fulfilment, but with the perceived immodesty that comes with writing a book about how happy you are.

It's true. I am one of the, if not the, happiest individual(s) I know — and I know this, not only by way of my own perception, but also of the perception of those around me, including both close friends and strangers, at times. Nonetheless, to publicly declare it in the form of publishing a book on the subject will always feel a little uncomfortable and awkwardly boastful to me.

I do not, however, think that there is any way around this other than to persevere and perhaps consider less of what others think, a lesson I have yet to fully implement in my day-to-day. Sometimes it's also just very good to be brave.

With that being said, I would like to start this book off with the conviction that not one person on this earth has the right to gatekeep happiness.

You see, my one life is mine, just as your one life is yours, and throughout the course of our respective lives, we are equally tasked with finding small ways to create joy as we wade through the chaos. Writing this book (and re-reading it many times) is one of my small ways, and perhaps reading it will become one of yours too.

We all want to be happy, but none of us were ever handed the guidebook. And while this fact can be unbelievably frustrating, it doesn't strike me as reason enough to give up, nor to resign ourselves to the idea that happiness is the result of sheer luck.

While it's not my place to decide the extent to which you view your happiness as your own responsibility, if given an option between a) utter powerlessness or b) the minor possibility of influence, then you can be sure I'm arguing in favour of the latter — and that this book will provide information (and hopefully the useful sort) accordingly.

This book is for anyone who already feels the same or is at least open-minded enough to allow me to attempt to change their mind. I think it's only fair to say that if you leave this experience feeling worse off and increasingly unhappy than you did when you arrived, I owe you your money back.

Let's begin.

Chapter 1 – Happiness Haves & Have Nots

They say that the thing you focus on is the thing that grows. In the case of happiness, there couldn't be a truer statement.

Happiness is an upward spiral. When leaned in to, it has the ability to exponentially reproduce itself and crop up in the areas of our life where we might not even expect it. You'll find yourself looking the mundane in the face with a smile, greeting a bad day with an extra dose of self-care, and reasoning with sheer disaster about the pros and cons of the bright side.

You'll come to notice how it's possible to infect people with your happiness, and sometimes you'll see it reflected back at yourself in the mirror, too. The sky will seem bluer, and the sun will feel warmer. All this to say, if you could purchase happiness over the counter, I assure you, it'd be one hell of a drug.

Most importantly, you will know that you are doing it right when it becomes one of the first things noticed about you by others.

~~Happy Ever After~~ Happy Now

I'm going to go ahead and say it: I don't believe happiness is elusive. Moreover, I don't believe that *believing* the idea that 'happiness is elusive' can ever be conducive to locating it.

Happiness is not something a small handful of lucky individuals just happen to stumble their way into one day — rather, it's the cumulative sum of one's thoughts, beliefs, habits, and behaviours. It's what you direct your attention towards, where you exert your energy, and which actions you choose to engage in routinely.

Your happiness does not exist in the ever after, with the number in your bank account, or with your next big promotion. Your happiness does not exist with your partner, your kids, or your group of best friends. There is precisely one place happiness exists — and it's inside of your brain.

Take it or leave it.

But unlike that quick dopamine hit you get when purchasing something online, *true* happiness is not something you can order to your front door with the click of a button. More akin to meditation than a simple switch to be flipped on again and off again, happiness is a concerted effort that requires practice and conscious decision-making.

I won't spoil the contents of the remainder of this book for you, but I will say that there is no one single reason why some people are happier than others — there are one thousand of them. From negative self-talk, to letting one's life be governed by fear, to not eating the right kinds of foods. From believing that life is out to get you, to becoming far too acquainted with the comfort zone. From perceiving happiness as something that you are owed, to failing to recognize it when it arrives, and to comparisons in all its forms.

All in all, there are many different ways to be miserable. It's about time together we found a few to make us happy.

Why I'm Happy & You're Not (If Only It Were That Simple)

I suppose it's only fair for me to share my experience first... being that I am what people describe as a *naturally happy person* and all.

Now, I write the following at the fully-internalised risk of sounding like a complete fool. Nobody ever wants to write full paragraphs about what a happy person they are. They just don't. The only reason I want to share this with you is because it's true and may be the only piece of writing I've never felt the desire to wildly embellish.

To begin, it's important to note that I was never instinctually aware of possessing this quality, nor committing to the habits and mental routines that encouraged my happy disposition, until a large enough number of people took it upon themselves to point it out to me.

It is also important to note that it is by no means the case that I happen to be surrounded by notably *un-happy*, negative people — because I'm not. It's just where others go about their day on a setting closer to normal, you can find me singing through the streets, dancing at the bus stop, and laughing at my own jokes and funny (to me) thoughts. Of course, this occurs quietly and very much in seclusion. Picture me happy, please, but not certifiable.

In addition, I am quite easily impressed, vastly casual with my laughter, and I often make my way through life in a world of my own. I can be clumsy too, but I find almost all of my errors to exist somewhere on the scale of life lessons to funny — and thankfully, mostly the latter in recent years.

My happiness doesn't only manifest itself in an obvious manner; rather, there are many distinct areas of my life where I see it showing up in both big and little ways...

I find beauty and absurdity in the most mundane of things and the very same things I observe others passing by unfazed. I have a penchant for conflict resolution, giving the benefit of the doubt, and I feel a strict responsibility to abide by my sense of moral right and wrong while still firmly embracing the notion of *live and let live.*

I also have a close friend who (in jest) believes my life is destined to favour a pendulum: the first half spent swinging happily on a conspicuous high, the second part propelling me towards an inevitable period of doom and gloom; the necessity of an equal but opposite reaction and all that (but more on that reckoning in Chapter 10).

I bring this up in this chapter because I gather that this is his *unique* way of explaining (and equalizing) my on-going happiness...The takeaway being, of course, that for most of my life, I have been told this is notably unusual. And, since becoming more acutely aware of it — I have to say that I'm beginning to agree.

I see how straightforwardly people give into their own frustration, how negatively my friends speak to themselves in passing as if it bears no weight at all, and how angry far too many individuals are at the world we all live in. Upsettingly, I do think most people are severely unhappy. And where happiness is a spiral that only goes up, misery is the fastest route to spiralling down.

But, as you'll read further on, I don't think life is meant to be all sunshine and roses, and I'm certainly not under any delusions about the state of our current existence. I also don't mean to suggest that I never experience bad moods, or problems of my own. I do, of course, and I'll detail exactly how I prefer to handle them further on.

It's just that with the right perspective, I believe we possess the ability to view (and feel) them as a whole lot less important than everything else in life.

Namely, that is, being able to live it *happily*.

Chapter 2 – Happy as the Chemicals in Your Brain

The biological and chemical processes that occur in the brain are responsible for all aspects of cognitive functioning, and what we define as the experience of happiness is no exception.

Here, our cells communicate using neurotransmitters, via synapses and synaptic gaps within the brain in order to determine our thoughts, behaviours, motivations, ability to learn and retain information, and even our mood.

There are, primarily, four neurotransmitters within the brain that concern themselves with our happiness. They are: dopamine, serotonin, oxytocin, and endorphins.

And while these complex chemical messengers play their respective roles in shaping our everyday emotions and reactions without requiring any additional supervision on our part, it's still us who are in control of the majority of input they receive.

So before we can begin to attribute our stubborn unhappiness to faulty wiring or mother nature's idea of a sick joke, we humans are first responsible (or at least we very much ought to be) for engaging in actions and interactions that are hard-wired to bring us delight.

In fact, simply by knowing when and how these neurotransmitters fire in our brains, we have the potential to use them to our great advantage.

It's like teaching the brain how to hack itself.

Neuro-ception, if you will.

(P.S. if neuroscience isn't your jazz and you can already feel your eyes glazing over, then know that this next chapter is only quick. There are some technical explanations and terms, but go slowly, and I assure you, you will survive. Try to conjure up two activities from each section that you realistically feel you could accomplish each day).

22 Brain Hacks to Happiness

Dopamine

This neurotransmitter is commonly referred to as the reward chemical — but it actually has a lot more to do with motivation than reward (1).

For example, if you were to measure the release of dopamine in the brain before, during, and after receiving a reward, you'd find that all activity of this particular neurotransmitter would come to a grinding halt as soon as that first taste of reward was experienced.

So, contrary to what is highlighted by many of the dopaminergic articles you may read (no? maybe, that's just me), research shows that the signaling of dopamine neither diminishes nor disappears, even when a reward is not attained. Rather, it was found that equal amounts of dopamine are released in an area of the brain known as the *nucleus accumbens* — both when a player loses a bet as well as when they win.

Thus, you'll find that particular activities such as gambling, where reward attainment is significantly unpredictable, have a tremendously more dramatic effect on your dopamine receptors than others where a reward is generally more guaranteed.

With that said, I'm not going to recommend you to turn to gambling as a way of hacking some extra dopamine. In fact, the real goal with dopamine is to maintain a healthy baseline level; not too much for your long-term motivation to suffer and/or crash and not too little to prevent you from actioning your goals in the first place.

To do this, try to mix and match some of the following activities (2):

1. Intermittently rewarding yourself for the completion of a task (the key is not every time!)

2. Viewing early morning sunlight for 10-30 minutes

3. Viewing or creating a piece of art

4. Having a snack or ingesting caffeine

5. Engaging in acts of 'self-care'

6. Having an orgasm

Serotonin

This neurotransmitter is implicated in the mediation of happiness, optimism, and general satisfaction — it's also the chemical thought to be responsible for depression when produced inadequately within the body (around 90% of this production actually takes place within the human digestive tract, aka the gut (3)).

(Don't worry, you'll be hearing plenty more from me in Chapter 14 about the role that food plays in supporting mental health).

In the meantime, you should know that serotonin also enhances the production of dopamine and simultaneously *inhibits* the production of cortisol — the unhappy hormone that's released from the adrenal glands and is associated with increased levels of stress, neuroticism, and depression (4).

By hampering the release of cortisol within the body, serotonin stabilizes the nervous system and allows for higher-order thinking skills like objectivity and rationality in decision-making to take place.

So, if you're feeling a little too overwhelmed or overstimulated by your current environment, give some of the following activities a go and observe how your happiness and peacefulness increase as a result:

7. Meditating

8. Getting some sun

9. Spending time in nature

10. Going for a run/bike/swim

11. Eating plant foods high in tryptophan

12. Visualizing a happy memory

Oxytocin

This powerful peptide hormone and happiness neurotransmitter is all about love. Responsible for the warm and fuzzy feeling we primarily associate with romantic satisfaction and physical touch, oxytocin is also linked to a range of social, behavioural, and physiological effects such as empathy, bonding between a mother and child, and the establishment of trust (5).

Evolutionarily speaking, we have an intrinsic need for security within our interpersonal relationships, as well as the acceptance and affection of our in-group (those that we consider being a part of a shared identity or sphere of interests). For this reason, oxytocin plays a large role in determining our overall happiness, as it facilitates our social interactions and largely encourages companionship (6).

Oxytocin is also the chemical compound found in MDMA — which explains why people report feeling more or less in love with everything in their general vicinity.

Aside from self-dosing with ecstasy, however (which, I admit, I've never tried and can therefore not sensibly recommend), it is possible to boost your levels of oxytocin in a variety of different ways. Consider the following:

13. Petting an animal

14. Interacting with a child

15. Holding someone's hand

16. Giving a 30-second hug

17. Complimenting someone

18. Listening to music

Endorphins

Technically speaking, endorphins are opioid peptides that act as neurotransmitters. But, unlike other neurotransmitters, they're produced by the central nervous system and have the primary function within the body to relieve and eliminate pain. In fact, endorphins are actually comparable to morphine in both their structure and the site where they bind to receptors within the brain — making them an endogenous (a.k.a. of natural internal origin) form of the very same drug (7).

Research shows that exercising, even something as manageable for most as 30 minutes of walking per day, is enough to significantly increase levels of endorphins and reap the benefits of a stronger, better, and more confident mood (8).

In addition to both aerobic and anaerobic forms of exercise, endorphins tend to kick in when a heightening of emotions is at play. This can include moments of intense fear, fits of laughter, and even a few types of indulgence.

Thus, when in need of boosting this pain-relieving happiness chemical, look no further than trying some of the following:

19. Watch something funny (or thrilling)

20. Using essential oils/soaking with Epsom salts

21. Eating some dark chocolate

22. Exercising

Now that you have a reference guide for these happiness hacks, start paying attention to the actions you spend more time on and, consequently, to the actions where you spend less. While none of the activities above can single-handedly provide you with happiness on a plate, they're certainly helpful to return to when you need some neurotransmitters to have your back.

Chapter 3 – Humans Evolved to Survive, Not to Necessarily be Happy About It

There is an unhelpful misconception that, as humans, we are entitled to this thing we call happiness. More or less, there exists the idea that happiness is our life's true purpose; the item we were sent to this earth to diligently locate — and that, in its absence, we have drastically failed.

Excuse my French, but how the hell did this become our raison d'être?

Sure, happiness may provide our lives with meaning; it's what we sentimentalize and covet in order to colour our days with a certain degree of purposefulness, but make no mistake, it is not what we were made for.

Just like every individual cell of our body, our sole existence is based on the drive to reproduce (and obviously survive long enough to do so), being prompted by our chemistry to select a mate with *particularly* good genes while we're at it.

Approximately 0% of our biological blueprint concerns itself with making sure we are happy.

Evolutionarily speaking, that would only seem like a great deal of wasted effort — an effort that could otherwise be distributed elsewhere far more important such as eating, sleeping, or having sex. (It sounds funny, but it's true). And once you learn to accept this fact of nature, ironically, happiness becomes significantly easier to attain.

The Great Evolutionary Mismatch

Evolutionary mismatch is a term typically used to describe the incompatibilities of our current environmental and lifestyle factors with the circumstances in which our genes and physiological traits first emerged (9).

Take, for example, the fact that the species we belong to, the *Homo sapiens*, evolved over 200,000 years ago — yet the majority of the human genome today looks exactly the same as it did back then.

This would be fine, in theory, had our lives continued to resemble those of our ancient ancestors.

In this case, the originally adaptive and helpful traits we gained via the process of natural selection all those years ago would currently still be operating in our favour.

Instead, we find ourselves — still nearly biologically identical to the earliest of *Homo sapiens* — but now faced with a plethora of modern technological developments in every corner and crevice of our day-to-day lives.

From the first moment that we open our eyes in the morning to the second that we close them again at night, our every interaction with the external world is characterized by a serious evolutionary discrepancy. Almost *every* aspect of how we live today would be completely alien to our ancestors — from the foods we eat to the ways we are most likely, statistically speaking, to die.

Biology doesn't stand the slightest chance of keeping up. The process of evolution is about several million times slower than the speed of a snail, and we humans are moving faster than ever.

This isn't a bad thing in and of itself — it's just a thing. What it does mean, however, is that the problems we currently face (as far as the pursuit of health, happiness, and fulfilment go) are ones our biology has not necessarily equipped us to solve…

Evolution, Happiness, and Physical Health

Physical health seems like a good place to start any conversation about happiness (not that I'm exactly starting it here, but you get the point) because until we can upload our consciousnesses to some dystopian version of The Cloud, we are required to live a physical life. And it doesn't take any great stretch of the imagination to suppose that your idea of a happy and blissful life is likely one that includes a distinct *lack* of physical suffering and pain.

If you think it's hard to find happiness living in a healthy body, then trust that living in an unhealthy one will really put a damper on your day.

So, we conclude that staying healthy is important — and perhaps especially so, as our evolutionary biology has such a strong tendency to try and trip us up.

You see, when our Late-Paleolithic era ancestors evolved, there were two prime aspects of their ancient lives that have continued to shape our relationship with health, even today. These were: 1) a drastically inconsistent supply of food, and 2) constant fluctuating cycles of physical activity versus rest due to their dependence on a hunger-gatherers lifestyle.

Not only are these two lifestyle factors inextricably linked in the case of both feast or famine, but the survival of our *Homo sapiens* predecessors would have depended on their ability to efficiently regulate the intake and storing of fuel. So when certain genes were selected for via the process of natural selection (i.e. the ones our bodies decided to keep) — these would have been those genes. And because our genes have barely shifted in over 200,000 years, it would be absurd to presume that anything has changed (10).

We are programmed biochemically to respond to cycles of food, no food, physical activity, and rest. So, what happens then when you pair that programming with our modern lifestyle of constant (processed, high calorie, high cholesterol) food and almost constant inactivity and rest?

Something along the lines of:

- Type 2 Diabetes
- Cardiovascular Disease
- Stroke
- Obesity

- Metabolic Disorders

These are our number 1, 2, and 3 top causes of death, and the list goes on. There is a severe evolutionary mismatch between the way our body thinks we live and the way we actually do. Is it any wonder why happiness seems that little bit harder to physically attain?

The Same but Mental

Just like physical health — but better — our mental health is one of those things we really need to prioritize in order to be happy. But, funnily enough, evolution doesn't really help us out there, either.

In reality, research suggests that nature's failure to weed out disorders such as anxiety and depression may arise from the reality that nature doesn't necessarily view these feelings as a bad thing.

Indeed, despite the obvious obstacles that depression poses on the rates of survival and reproduction for *Homo sapiens*, depression is viewed by natural selection as a useful adaption and one that prevents us from staying in risky or perceivably hopeless situations (11, 12).

Fascinatingly, an extensive research study of the Kaluli hunter-gatherer tribe in the highlands of New Guinea found that only *one* individual out of the thousands assessed even came close to meeting the diagnostic criteria for clinical depression (13). By comparison, depression is reported to affect over 18% of the US population per year — making that number closer to 400 for every 2000 Americans (14).

There's no question as to whether or not depression is real, but there may be a wealth of sociocultural factors in modern life (and not that of hunter-gatherer communities) that contribute to the experience of depression as a disorder instead of a mere disposition.

"The most fundamental issue, and also the most contentious one, is whether disease and illness are normative concepts based on value judgments, or whether they are value-free scientific terms; in other words, whether they are biomedical terms or sociopolitical ones (15)." ~
R.E. Kendell

Here, evolutionary mismatch is to blame for our mental disturbances, just as much as it is for our physical ones; quite frankly, humans have evolved to survive but not necessarily to be happy about it.

While I'm not necessarily sure what to do with this information exactly, I do feel that, at the very least, it helps to take away some of the pressure.

We're not failing because we're an unhappy species — it's likely that because we still exist as a species *at all*, happiness can feel so goddamn hard to find.

Thankfully, that doesn't mean that it is.

Chapter 4 – How to Re-wire Your Brain to Feel Happier, Easier

Before we get into the nitty-gritty of cultivating happiness, there are three myths that concern the way in which our brains work that we need to get out of the way:

Myth 1: That our brains don't change once we enter adulthood

Myth 2: That we can separate psychological disorders from physiological ones

Myth 3: That *you* are the same thing as your mind

Now, although it may be true that the hardware of our brain stops developing right around the time we reach our mid-to-late twenties, we retain the ability to shape and sculpt certain areas long after they are initially established.

This concept, something referred to as neural-plasticity, explains the permanent malleability of the human brain that can range from taking place on a teeny-tiny cellular level, all the way up to a large-scale rewiring of the way we think, operate, and subsequently *live* every single day.

Think about the last time you chose to take a new route to work; it probably required some studying of the passing road signs, as well as paying increased attention to any unfamiliar traffic lights, stop signs, or pedestrian crossings you might inadvertently otherwise miss.

Now, what if I told you that you would have been physically altering the structure of your brain by doing so?

What if I said that with every new left or right turn you took, your brain would begin to piece together the stimuli of your whereabouts and actively start to rewire itself in order to accommodate the new and incoming information?

The truth is that anytime we see, hear, or do something new, our brains construct new neural pathways that allow us to engage in the process we call learning.

Something as simple as taking a different route to work one day can enable an expansion of our cognitive map (i.e. the mental map that appears when we picture the way to get to the living room, work, or school) and forge new chemical links between these old and new places as they exist in our minds.

And, fascinatingly, the neural pathways in our brain – the ones responsible for forging these chemical links involved in the learning process – can look very, very different depending on how often we use them.

The ones we use the most are broad and expansive (think: a highway of rush hour traffic), while the ones we use less are narrow and thin (think: a weedy garden path). The ones we don't use at all get closed off after a certain amount of inactivity; the brain *is* wired for efficiency, after all.

Thinking Patterns Can Change Your Brain

Neural pathways, as well as our wide range of neurotransmitters, both have an awful lot to do with the way our brain communicates with itself. These chemical hormones, such as serotonin, dopamine, oxytocin, norepinephrine, etc., all play a very serious role in the regulation of our mental and physical health.

In this sense, our brain chemistry can have a direct impact on how we think and how we feel every day, just like we discussed a couple of chapters back. However, it's important to note that the inverse is also true: how we think and feel everyday can also have a direct physiological impact on the chemistry of our brains.

Now, in order to bridge this information with the discussion of happiness, we initially need to understand what happens to the brain when a person suffers from a shortage of it, i.e., depression.

There are two particular areas of the brain that become altered in an individual with depression. The *amygdala* — the part that controls our fear and fight-or-flight response — is found to increase in size, and the *hippocampus* — the control center for the regulation of our emotions — is found to decrease and get smaller in size (16).

What's *most* fascinating about this, though, is that research has shown that following psychological treatment for depression, and a reduction in negative thinking patterns, our hippocampus actually possesses the ability to regrow in size (and, therefore, optimal function) (17).

What this means is that no matter whether a state of unhappiness is brought on by chemical factors or situational ones (such that can be seen with disorders like depression), there is an inextricable link between our thinking patterns and the physical wiring of our brains... So much so, in fact, that we possess the ability to regain key regulatory functions of the brain, just by no longer struggling with the mental by-products of a disorder (i.e. negative thoughts).

Long story short – your thinking patterns really can change your brain!

The Power of Awareness

Next, it's important to understand that there is a difference between your mind and the awareness you have of your mind:

You are not your mind.

You are not even your awareness.

You are the thing paying attention to it.

And guess what? If you can understand how the mind works and how to positively use the power of attention, then you can harness all its abilities in order to improve yourself, your life, and your overall happiness.

Let's try something. An experiment.

Take a second and try to imagine that your mind is a vast space with many different areas or rooms (maybe like a house, or a hotel). Each of these rooms represents a different emotion and a different set of neural pathways responsible for processing that emotion. There's a room for sadness, a room for happiness, a room for fear, joy, anger, desire, frustration, hope, and anything else that comes to mind.

Now try to imagine your awareness as it exists in your mind.

You can think of it as a ball of light. This light can freely wander in the hotel and can provide energy to any of the rooms it goes into. As a result, it feeds those neural pathways and strengthens them. Making the journey into that specific room and the path to that specific emotion feels a lot simpler every time light enters the room.

When your awareness — your light — goes to any one of these areas of the mind, it lights up that area, and you become conscious of being in that area. Are *you* angry? No — you are not your mind. But your awareness is lighting up your anger area, and suddenly you become aware of being angry.

The same exact thing applies to happiness, sadness, and all the other emotions too.

The power here is that you can use willpower and the art of conscious thought to move your awareness/ball of light into any of the rooms you please. Wherever awareness goes, is where your energy goes, is where your neural pathways get stronger, is where you are more likely to go the next time.

This becomes problematic when we allow our circumstances, or perhaps the people around us, to dictate where our awareness is going. When this happens, our energy gets restricted to that one particular area, and we've relinquished our power of thought to factors outside of our control.

How can we really be surprised, then, when consequently, we no longer feel like happiness is a personal choice?

In this case, we've already decided it's not.

Understand that controlling your awareness = controlling your emotions = controlling how your brain responds to the world around you, moving forward.

Re-wiring Our Brains to be Happier

Now if we interpret (notice I use the word interpret) a particular moment to be stressful or threatening, our brain releases adrenaline and cortisol to try and give us the tools to help us survive.

The trouble is that when our bodies react to these chemicals being produced, we experience physiological discomfort (symptoms such as sweaty palms, increased heart rate, and raised blood pressure) that, in turn, makes us feel even more stressed and out of sorts.

This process reinforces itself — thanks, neural connections! — thus creating a cycle of stress. It makes sense, then, that individuals suffering from depression often have heightened levels of these chemicals floating around in their brain.

But what if we were to take this understanding and apply it to the experience of positive emotions instead?

Let's say we were able to reframe the situation to instead be interpreted (there's that word again) as being not so stressful. If we could somehow switch our perspective on this event and see it as something *exciting* rather than anxiety-inducing – then we might be able to convince our brain to release less of these stress hormones.

Less of these hormones means less sweating and a lower heart rate… and a lower heart rate means fewer physiological signals to our body that we have anything to be nervous about.

This is where our thinking patterns come in. They hold the key to the *how* of re-wiring our brains for happiness.

When we begin thinking negative thoughts, for instance, and we give our attention to the areas of our mind that contain anger, sadness, and unhappiness, the neural pathways that transmit those messages become strengthened, and the tendency for repetition or habituation of these negative thoughts becomes increased as our brains seek the path of least resistance (i.e. our brains gravitate towards the big open highways, not the weedy garden paths).

On the other hand, when we consciously make an effort to perceive a situation as positive, and to direct our attention, our light, to the rooms in our mind that contain joy, gratitude, and happiness, then these become the rooms we are more likely to return to again.

By shifting our thoughts into helpful, productive ones instead of destructive ones, we make sure that the neural connections specific to happiness will be the ones that get to feed and grow stronger from our energy. We make sure that *these* are the rooms we are more likely to visit with our light when the going gets rough and that we can fall back on during times of temporary unhappiness or depression.

Planning For Unhappiness

Don't get me wrong, there is no shortcut to avoiding unhappiness — and anyone who tries to tell you otherwise is quite simply just wasting your time.

There will be times of catastrophe, uncertainty, and even monumental pain. It's *life*, after all.

All we can really hope for is to find a way to minimize the unhappy moments and maximize the happy ones. In this sense, making sure that we've done as much of the heavy lifting involved in the task of re-wiring our brain as possible before our circumstances try to knock us off our feet; highly recommended.

To begin with, we ought to, in fact, be building up these neural pathways to happiness by practising the art of conscious positive thinking when we're feeling happy, strong, loved, and successful, *not* when we're trying to find a quick fix for a bad day.

By taking small moments of inconvenience or upset on the chin and by choosing to shine your light of awareness on the positive of the situation even when it's tempting to do the opposite, you are giving your brain a chance to default to the path of happiness the next time when it may otherwise be just that small bit more difficult.

Time is going to pass whether we make good use of it or not, so we might as well use it to make our future selves just that little bit better, being happy.

In essence, do try to think more positively; it may just change your life.

Chapter 5 – The Care Guide for Happiness (Batteries Not Included)

The Necessity of Knowing Thy Self

I don't know how you're supposed to be happy.

Okay, in the general sense, sure—I can explain what it might take for you (a nondescript human being) to be happy. But ultimately, I can't tell you much about *you*. The unique you. The you who will have a different sense of humour, a different gorgeous amalgamation of goals and fears, and an altogether completely different set of brain chemistry than me.

I mean, only you can do that, which is why it's so important for both of us that you understand exactly who you're dealing with here.

Moreover: *who are you, and what makes you happy?*

It's okay if you don't have the perfect answer to this yet. Even if you do, give it a couple of months, and it's bound to change, and that's perfectly okay too. What is key, however, is that you commit yourself to always finding out— and if that means changing the way you live your life in order to cater to the specific things that makes you happy, then so be it.

Subsequently, once you know exactly who you are, it's important to be exactly who you are.

Countless self-help books advertise their ability to transform you into a richer, handsomer, funnier, *happier* type of person, and maybe the type of person who wakes up at 5 am or prefers sleeping for 3-hour intervals scheduled throughout the day instead. The point is that there are self-help books on being most anything and everything.

The problem with books like these is that their premises rest on the assumption that first, you must do or be *better* to achieve the optimal you. On the contrary, in this chapter, I propose leaning **into the idea that, first, in order to be better, the single most important thing you have to be is *you*.**

The truth of the matter is that we could all use being a bit more *something*, and a bit less *something else.* We all have things that can be improved upon—I mean, across the board, that's probably a fair statement to make—but that's not exciting, interesting, or new.

Alternatively, the thing with the most power to make a difference day-to-day has a lot more to do with the extent to which we honor our authentic selves and maintain our integrity.

Research shows that individuals who possess greater insight — i.e., heightened levels of intuitive understanding of themselves and the world around them — also experience higher levels of relationship satisfaction, happiness, self-acceptance, and overall sense of life purpose, among other positive things (18).

So, to lead by example and encourage you to gain and little more understanding and insight about yourself, I'm going to share a little about me.

Introvert, Extrovert, Ambivert, Happy

A good friend once described me as strangely down-to-earth for someone with her head so perpetually up in the clouds. I remember laughing, feeling both amused at his creative thought as well as delightedly taken aback by the feeling of being so well summed up in so few words. It always feels nice to be *got*.

You see, if you're a person, like me, who can relate to walking the personality line between being an introvert and an extrovert, then you know all too well the feeling of existing in a space somewhere between the thoughts in your head and the external world.

Sometimes happiness can feel like completely different things on different days. Learning to embrace my inclination towards ambiversion is just one of the ways I'm trying to accept the fact that no one is responsible for protecting my happiness but me.

In this case, both introversion and extroversion (two characteristics on polar opposite sides of the spectrum) have been widely studied within psychology as a core determinate of behavioural and cognitive outcomes such as job performance, positive social interactions, and the risk of developing mood abnormalities, like depression (19).

According to the psychological theory of the Big Five, these traits also comprise one of the five overall aspects of an individual personality.

In other words, knowing where you fall on the scale of introversion vs. extroversion might provide you with a wealth of benefits when it comes to taking care of your happiness and looking after yourself.

As a 22-year-old who has spent the past four years of her adolescence-to-adulthood experience in one of the most fast-paced, bustling, and buzzing cities of the world, I've come to learn some things about managing my time, inter-personal relationships, and work-play-life balance in a way that preserves both my mental health as well as my emotional sanity.

As we're all just trying to navigate the hairy junctions between the ups and downs of living our best life, it's my hope that these tried and tested tips and tricks can help you as much as they do me.

Hello, fellow ambiverts; this one is for you! And to the die-hard introverts and extroverts: should the following advice not quite hit the spot, consider taking some time with yourself to come up with your own bespoke guide to caring for your best and happiest self.

1. Don't Over-schedule Yourself

I feel that I owe myself an explanation for why exactly it is that over-scheduling my own week/day/month/year appears to be one of my preferred sources of adrenaline.

It's the feeling where you question whether or not you remember the correct number of hours in each day — was I thinking it was 30? 45? Dear God Jesus, you're telling me there are only 24?!

Well, whether these commitments are personal, professional, or in the likely case of both being true, ambiverts such as myself have a high tendency to over-schedule themselves. While certainly half of the time, we might crave interaction and experience FoMO at the thought of any fun or interesting plans being made in our absence, we may also become all too easily overwhelmed by the idea of facing a full day of social obligations without any downtime or moments of solitude to ourselves.

This is no way to encourage mindful happiness.

Thus, the key takeaway (for myself, and anyone who can relate) is to learn not to over-schedule oneself. Remember that there's always the chance to make new plans if you find yourself with extra time and social energy on your hands. In fact, when it comes to productivity — an important component of overall life satisfaction — research shows that being constantly surrounded by others is one of the fastest ways to not only take more time in completing tasks at hand, but also to perform worse, in general (20).

Your future self may thank you for thinking of your quieter, less ambitiously-overeager introverted side for once. So, guard your happiness and solitude fiercely, and look out for the less exposed dimensions of your personality, too.

2. Set your Intention for the Week(s) Ahead

Not entirely dissimilar to my previous point: know that strategically organizing your head space is no less important than strategically organizing your calendar. This becomes especially important for ambiverts when it comes to mentally preparing one's duality of mind for whatever the week ahead may bring.

If you know you have people to see, plans to be made, and events to attend, it may benefit you in the long term to remind yourself what you hope to get out of the next few hours, days, or even weeks.

The benefits of quiet visualisation, and time spent alone, are well documented to include improved stress management, slower perceived pace of life, greater stability of mental health, and one interesting quality referred to by psychologists as 'strength of mind' (21).

By taking a moment to reflect on our intentions and short-term future goals, we perhaps mitigate the inevitable back and forth with our brain on whether to stay in or go out, or whether to meet friends or have a 1-on-1 meeting with Netflix instead.

I know for me, even just giving my introverted side the heads-up about the socially busy week ahead or allowing my extroverted half to come to terms with a few days of cracking on with a solo work assignment makes me feel a lot more cared for, and happy as a whole.

3. Learn to Ask for Alone Time

An increasing amount of research shows that being able to spend some good old-fashioned one-on-one time with yourself is linked to improved life satisfaction, elevated levels of creativity, and more rewarding social interactions, amongst other positive (and happiness multiplying) outcomes (22).

With that being said, it can be much easier said than done. You see, asking for *Me-time* is not something that comes even remotely naturally to me.

Do I often want alone time? Yes.

Do I often need alone time? Yes.

Do I know how to politely explain to those around me that I need this aforementioned alone time? Not yet...

But I'm working on it!

And you should, too, because you can never get anything without asking. And knowing when you've drained your extroversion battery for the day is just as much about looking after yourself as it is about looking out for those around you. I remember when it first dawned on me that maybe I should be communicating my needs for some solitary reflection *before* they become glaringly apparent — oops!

Nobody likes a moody ambivert on the wrong side of social interaction. Learning to talk or text the words, "I'm taking some alone time to unwind," into existence will help us all in the pursuit of happiness, I swear.

4. Get Out of Your Head & into Your Body

There are times I can feel my extroversion leading the way: I say borderline hilarious things without pondering them for ten minutes beforehand, I talk to strangers in public without thinking twice, and I seem to walk around this city of mine with a certain degree of happy-go-lucky pizzazz.

Other times this is quite simply not the case: I can feel myself getting stuck in a 'think-y' mood of sorts, and the stimuli of the external world seems altogether too bright, too loud, and too much.

It's not necessarily a bad thing — these moments just have the propensity to make me crave the freedom to turn inwards and just be me for a while. *Oh, hi introversion; it's so nice to see you again.*

But what's an ambivert like me to do when in need of switching gears?

Well, the trick that always seems to work for me when I'm in need of a quick way to snap out of my introversion is exercise! I can dance, run, work out, or even just flail around the room for a bit in a process I like to refer to as 'getting into your body.'

If I had to guess the science behind this and why it works, I'd argue that it's not too dissimilar to the way that shaking or vibrating the body is thought to reduce tension and anxiety by returning the nervous system to its neutral, homeostatic state.

As silly as it sounds, there's something about raising the rate of my heartbeat in a very physical way that does wonders for coaxing my social enthusiasm and joie de vivre out of hibernation – or, at the very least, placating my social anxiety.

5. Give Yourself Time to Think

Take it from me; spacing out in the middle of a busy high street in London tends to result in a collision, amongst other unpleasant things. I'm not proud to admit that I've been known to walk into trees, lamp posts, and even innocent bystanders at times when too caught up in my own thoughts to pay adequate attention to my surroundings. (For everyone's sake, I hope not all happy people are as dizzy).

I've also noticed that this issue becomes further exacerbated when there's something, in particular, I'm in need of thinking about, whether a concept for a new article, thoughts on how I may phrase the concluding paragraph of a very important email, or even just the mental reflection of recent conversation — as any number of these ideas could be buzzing around my brain at any given moment.

To accompany this, I often feel an enormous amount of pressure to organize and plan, and when I don't proactively allocate myself *enough* time to do so, I end up sacrificing precious 'live in the moment' moments for some half-assed introverted introspection.

That, and there's also evidence to suggest that small, but frequent, moments of time taken to think and check in with oneself throughout the day are connected with a deepening of the relationship with oneself, as well as the increased ability to behave in a balanced manner, self-regulate one's mood, and enrich individual perspective-taking capabilities (23).

Therefore, I feel we should all give ourselves time to scribble down the notes we need to remember, sit for 15 minutes with a coffee, and get ourselves to a place where we can relax without stressing over our un-thunk thoughts. It's a game changer I will forever swear by, and it may save you countless hours trying to track down happiness in the long run.

6. Give Yourself Time to Decide

In a similar vein, try compelling your extroverted side of self to calm down with rapid-fire decision-making. In fact, I would go as far as to caution that it's necessary for ambiverts to exhibit a certain degree of caution when it comes to making up our plans, just as we ought to in making up our minds.

There's absolutely nothing wrong with telling your friends, "I'm going to think about it and get back to you if that's okay," or "I'm not actually sure I can commit to that yet. Can I give you an answer by Friday?"

Yet, somehow, becoming aware of this was quite the epiphany for me!

And so long as you're not just arbitrarily delaying your obligations and you actually stick to your word, others will only respect you all the more for knowing your own decision-making limitations.

So, pause — I know part of you (me) wants to have six social plans set up by sundown, but I also know that another part of you (we) might appreciate it if we increase our selectivity just a tad, and maybe go over the pros and cons of leaving the house that day... for the sake of saving your future, potentially socially-depleted self.

7. Accept the Duality of Your Personality, and Others will too

If you live in a place where you're all too familiar with the notion of a rat race— or even if you just have friends that lean more towards full-on extroversion than yourself — you'll understand that plans are always there to be made and that even when it feels like you're the only one out of your entire social group that feels the need to go on hiatus for a solid month or two, it's okay to accept yourself exactly the way you are.

We all have quirks, ticks, and buttons, and life is just a process of learning to navigate them while trying to have a good time while we're at it. If you take any one thing away from this chapter, I hope it's the confidence to internalize that the sooner you begin to care for your own mental well-being and happiness, the sooner everyone else will too.

So, hey, you fellow ambiverts, go out there and kick some ass — or maybe stay inside with a book — because you should know that's very okay, too.

Chapter 6 – Stop Letting Unfortunate Events Control Your Emotions

Some time ago, I spontaneously decided to download a daily gratitude app onto my iPhone because, you know, self-improvement— there is always something new to learn—and all that...

The app completed its download, I clicked it open, and was met with the smiling face of a flower-crown adorned llama prompting me with the question:

"What is the most optimistic interpretation of this situation?"

Okay. I see what you're trying to do here, smiling llama. The so-called 'bright side of things' is presumably always a nice place to be, and looking at it certainly seems like a reasonable place to start.

I immediately closed the app and went to sleep, making plans to delete it the following morning. I don't know what exactly I had in mind, but I don't need an app just to tell me to be more optimistic.

Thanks, but *no thanks*.

Fast forward to the early afternoon of the following day, and I had tasked myself with watering the collection of 30+ houseplants that decorate the various tabletops, bookshelves, and windowsills of my apartment.

I'll spare you all the riveting details of this endeavour, but you ought to know that there are three specific houseplants of mine that need to be taken onto the balcony for the water to drain fully, so as to avoid over-watering — it's a serious art this whole indoor gardening thing, I tell you.

Anyway, long story short, it happened to be a particularly windy day today, and in the 10 seconds that I turned my back on my 6ft tall Swiss Cheese plant, a gust of air had toppled it, sending its soil flying and its foliage crumbling under the weight of its own vine.

Now, watching this occur as it happened from less than 2ft away, I spun on my heels and tried to jump to its rescue, only to ram my full foot of toes into the porcelain of a nearby plant pot, sending it smashing into the balcony door where it proceeded to shatter into a pile of broken pieces.

Houseplants 1, Alex 0.

Feeling the sheer hopelessness (and physical pain) of the situation beginning to sink in, I thought I might cry. Suddenly then, from the depths of my distress, I heard a voice (thankfully my own) say,

"What is the most optimistic interpretation of this situation?"

I had to laugh.

I wasn't just laughing because smiling llama's words of wisdom had made an unexpected, but nonetheless appreciated, reappearance — although that was a key part of the reason — but I was laughing because *what the* hell *is the most optimistic interpretation of this situation?*

You know what I came up with at that moment? As utterly ridiculous as it sounds?

- My Swiss Cheese plant got to experience what it feels like to fly

- I have gone from having only one piece of the plant pot to having twelve

- The nerve endings in my toes all work, and that's a relief, I suppose

- At the very least, I think I learned a valuable lesson

Not only was my anger and frustration immediately dissolved by my own absurd sense of humour at that moment, but the sheer audacity of the smiling llama to actually contribute something in the way of self-help was admittedly rather admirable.

My toes were still sore hours after I pondered this, but, if you'll have me, I'd like to share with you some of the science behind why this one simple question has the power to stop allowing your unfortunate circumstance to control you.

The Smiling Llama Science

There is one key principle that lies at the heart of Cognitive Behavioural Therapy (CBT), and that is the way you think determines how you feel and how you behave.

Put differently, think of it as the notion that your thoughts directly translate to your feelings, which then directly translate to your behaviours — in turn, shaping your happiness, fulfilment, and associated life outcomes.

Now, we already know via our existence as human beings that our feelings and behaviours can be incredibly difficult to change. This is why it may come as good news that we really only need to focus on changing our *thoughts,* with the understanding that our *feelings* and *behaviours* will naturally be altered as a result.

This was partially what we covered in Chapter 4, with a focus on the physical, and neurological changes that take place in the brain when we begin to reframe our thoughts about a particular person, thing, or situation. So, for the time being, we're going to focus more specifically on the value of the question itself.

That is, *"What is the most optimistic interpretation of this situation?"*

Allow me to break down the three reasons why asking yourself this question works uniquely to alter your thoughts and re-wire your brain:

Interrupting your automatic response to the immediate circumstance creates space for rational, non-reactive thought to occur.

By engaging the brain to problem-solve (aka, finding creative ways to answer the question), you actively disengage your fight or flight response.

While the brain may be the most highly impressive organ, there are limits to what it can process in a single moment. If you've ever asked a screaming toddler, "what's that?" in an effort to distract them from their own meltdown, then you already know how powerful a simple re-directing of attention can be.

The precise phrasing of the question allows for perspective-taking — a proven way to increase empathy and prosocial behaviour, even towards oneself.

When we shift the focus from how *we* might feel toward the current reality to the way that an extreme optimist might perceive the same unfortunate situation, we effectively take on the role of the optimist for ourselves.

What's more, is that instead of being instructed by someone else to look on the bright side of things — an action that would no doubt trigger our defence mechanisms to fiercely object — we are harmlessly faced with a question we have posed to ourselves. We view this as a *challenge*, not a command, and it, therefore, aids us in our mission greatly.

Last but not least, it is psychologically impossible for gratitude and anxiety to co-exist.

A feat of mother nature, if you ask me, is that we are physically not capable of worrying about the same things we're busy being thankful for.

So, thank the fallen Swiss Cheese for remaining *mostly* intact.

Thank the broken plant pot for the four really good years of prior use it gave to you.

Thank the nerve endings in your toes for not only doing their job but also for reminding you that a big part of being alive is learning to walk (stroke hobble) through the pain.

And finally, thank the smiling llama for giving you the tools to control your emotions when things inevitably go wrong (because they definitely, definitely will)!

Chapter 7 - How to Calm Your Anxiety Using Only Your Eyes

Anxiety, while perhaps not in direct opposition to the experience of happiness, is certainly not conducive to it. Not only does a flood of hormones such as cortisol and adrenaline get released when we're anxious, but we often become prompted to do only one of three options: run away, face the danger head-on, or, in certain cases, completely freeze.

This is known, fittingly, as the flight, fight, or freeze response — or the fight-or-flight response as it's sometimes also called — and it's not exactly something you can easily (or without great sacrifice) multitask.

Fight, fight, or freeze is our body's way of protecting us in situations we perceive to be a threat to our survival (and do note the word 'perceived' here, as it's key).

So, while this mechanism may have first emerged as a way for our ancient ancestors to assess risks, such as coming face-to-face with an angry lioness or waging war with a neighbouring tribe, it's not uncommon for us to experience these same physiological reactions for slightly less formidable reasons like:

- giving a presentation
- going on a first date
- large social events
- thinking worrisome thoughts
- minor health issues
- simple confrontation

Because although these events aren't threats to our immediate survival, our brain doesn't quite know the difference — and can still perceive them as though they very much are. (As you'll recall from earlier, this isn't the first way evolutionary mismatch can trip us up when it comes to our search for ever-more happiness).

When our bodies react to the stress chemicals consequently produced, we experience physiological discomfort, with symptoms such as sweaty palms, increased heart rate, and raised blood pressure that, in turn, can make us feel even more stressed and out of sorts.

It becomes a negative spiral of anxiety, and it contributes to the feeling of being totally out of control while also being unable to redirect one's attention elsewhere. And there's that emphasis on your *power of attention*, once again.

In fact, this is where the phrase 'tunnel vision' comes from, and for anyone who's ever suffered from panic attacks, you'll know it's not a very pleasant one.

This is because tunnel vision has a very simple but profound effect on the eyes, and that is: they do not move. They become locked into whatever the current perceived threat may be, drawing more and more attention to that singular thing.

Consider that it's perhaps the most basic rule of survival to *not look away* from the angry, approaching lion.

Sometimes Seeing Is Believing

Now imagine the opposite of being super stressed and anxious and try to think of what might happen specifically to the movement of the eyes.

Are they fixated on one singular thing?

No. They're more likely zoning in and out, moving side-to-side, and taking in all the beautiful scenery...

just generally doing their eyeball thing. Think of the ways your eyes move when you're taking a stroll in the park, for example. Part of the essential process here (and you'll notice this next time you walk anywhere, for sure) has to do with forward motion.

When you walk forward, you pass things by. What this means is that things that were once front and centre to your line of vision slowly but surely make their way into your peripheral and eventually disappear entirely behind.

This forward movement of walking, paired with the natural tendency of the eyes to scan, effectively results in a side-to-side motion of the eyes. (On the contrary, remember that the opposite occurs when you are stressed. From an evolutionary perspective you wouldn't want to be peeling your eyes off of the angry lion — let alone letting it sneak somewhere behind you — so your eyes are much more likely to be locked).

Incredibly, this relaxed, side-to-side motion of the eyes has the ability to almost instantly quiet the response of the amygdala and sympathetic nervous system (24). Simply put, research shows that it gently but effectively shuts down the areas of your brain responsible for putting you in a flight, fight, or freeze response — rapidly decreasing your anxiety and fearfulness as a result.

But still... for the longest time, researchers couldn't figure out why walking forward was also implicated in this unique calming response.

On some levels, it makes sense. For example, you're probably less likely to take a stroll in the middle of a war zone, so surely walking means you must be pretty relaxed. The thing is, the threat detection centre of our brains — the amygdala, as we know — isn't connected to any of our limbs *at all*. How on earth, then, could it be capable of receiving a signal as to whether we're in forward motion or not?

The secret (again) has everything to do with the eyes.

Somethings Ancient, Somethings New

We now know for a fact that the amygdala is extremely aligned with the movement of the eyes, and, come to find out, it can receive the signal that we're on a walk, strictly because of the way we view our surroundings while moving forward.

As a result, walking, reading, or taking five minutes to move your eyes from side to side is legitimately all it takes to suppress the amygdala and initiate an effective calming response.

Lateralized eye movement as it's referred to in neuroscience.

However, the science doesn't end there. There's a second reason why the movement of the eyes has the outcome of generating a hugely beneficial, stress-reducing effect, and it's something that would have happened if our ancient ancestors were to select a different course of evolutionary action in the face of a threat.

Something that still happens in our brains to this day when, instead, we don't freeze; we choose that second option: to fight.

For the sake of continuity, let's say you're facing the lion once more. You've sized it up and determined that it's only a young one; it's got a rather ghastly injury on its left paw, and, as a bonus, let's say it stole the caribou you had been hunting for dinner. You're now faced with the choice to fight the lion or starve — and you decide to take your chances with the fight.

You would run towards it with everything you've got. Physically speaking, your limbs may move you forward the same way that they allow you to move on a walk; the difference is that, in this case, you are now on a strict physiological mission to survive.

Neurological research shows that moving forward into confrontation, and leaning into aggression, activates the dopamine reward pathway in the brain — the same chemical circuit linked to courage, boldness, motivation, and the desire to win (25).

In other words, we are rewarded, in turn, for our decision to face the threat, as well as chemically encouraged to overcome it. Our choice to handle a stressful event, despite the friction we experience from it, makes us *feel genuinely good.*

After all, this was once precisely how we survived.

Take this and pair it with the movement of the eyes as you go for a walk, run, or decide to read a book — anything that moves the eyes side-to-side (unfortunately, closed, or up and down doesn't work) — and you have a fool-proof way of not only unlocking some dopamine, but also immediately bringing your levels of anxiety down.

So, while there are some somewhat unkind processes instilled in our biological systems by mother nature, there are also some incredibly cool hacks for less stress (and more happiness), all to do with moving your eyes.

Chapter 8 – Find Out What You're Afraid Of, Then Do That Thing

Enough of lions. When I was five years old, I remember being afraid to go to the counter at a fast-food restaurant. There was a chain that would allow its customers to exchange any kid's toy included with the meal for a vanilla soft-serve ice cream cone. It was the first thing I can consciously remember being afraid of. (The exchange, not the ice cream).

I didn't want to have to go alone, I didn't want to do something wrong, and I certainly didn't want to set any new precedents with my parents — after all, being five years old had many a perk, and not being responsible for myself was largely one of them.

I remember my mum saying to me, "they're just a person, just like you or me, and the worst thing they can say to you is no."

Well damn, when you put it like that, mum.

But she was right — not just in the meaning of the words she was saying to me — but in knowing exactly what I needed to hear at that particular moment in time as I found my kid self at the crossroads of a very scary decision.

Somehow knowing that the only two possible outcomes of this venture were the person at the counter either saying 'yes,' and rewarding me with my treat, or saying 'no,' and leaving me empty-handed was enough.

Suddenly, it became a risk I was willing to take — I could handle not getting an ice cream if that was the worst *possible* thing to come from it, I thought.

Spoiler alert: I got my ice cream.

When I think back on the moments of my life that felt scary at first, only to give way to a plethora of positive outcomes shortly thereafter, I am reminded that what might *look* formidable and fear-inducing in their approach often were non-threatening when seen through the rear-view mirror we call hindsight. In other words, I'm no longer afraid of going to the counter all by myself, nor of the thousands of other things that once made my heart speed up, my palms sweat, and my voice tremble in mere contemplation of them all.

Someone once explained it to me in a way that permanently altered the course I viewed fear, and it goes like this: everything you currently have in life, whether it's your job, your house, or the friendships you currently maintain, are inside of your comfort zone. Logically, then, it follows that everything you *want* but *don't currently have*, exists in the space outside that zone. With a basic math equation, it becomes clear that in order to attain the things you want and to improve the life you're living, there is (and always will be) the inevitable requirement of stepping outside of your comfort zone.

Now, I'm not here to tell you that every opportunity to face your fears is going to be as simple or straightforward as ordering ice cream at the counter for the first time, but I am trying to say that it's worth it — irrevocably, and unequivocally — it will always be worth it.

On the Feeling of Fear

Fear is built into our evolutionary hard-wiring as human beings. Think about it. Fear is what keeps you alive, keeps you sharp, and keeps you fighting for the life you want to have. It is not an enemy but a superpower the moment you know how to harness it right.

The idea that you should be striving to reach a point of fearlessness is flawed for more than one reason. Firstly, it's not possible — we live in a rapidly evolving world with a near-constant onslaught of challenges and fears that have the capacity to surface with less than a moment's notice. Life is scary, and the sooner you accept that fact, the less power life has to scare you in the first place.

However, by examining the things that terrify you the most in the light of day, instead of allowing their shifting shadows to paralyze you with the fear of the unknown in the night, you reclaim ownership of your own psyche and control of your comfort.

Secondly, fearlessness is not something to aspire to, even if it were something possible to achieve one day. If you were truly fearless, you'd have nothing to gain, learn from, or grow. Your comfort zone would include everything under the sun, and it would be a rude wake-up call when you realize that life isn't about *having* things but about *experiencing* them.

And facing your fears is just that — facing them.

It's looking them in the eye and having a conversation with them. What are they there for? When did they get there, exactly? And what's the worst thing that could happen if we were to run towards them? Heart speeds up, palms start to sweat, voice trembles. That's awfully predictable, fear, I thought, you were far more dreadful than that.

And while we're at it, we should learn to recognize the signs of fear and use them to evaluate the situation at hand. These are our options:

Option A: Fear that is there to keep you safe. Pay attention to your surroundings and get yourself out of all immediate danger. Look both ways when you cross the road, don't walk alone at night, leave your drink unattended, and don't climb into the lion enclosure at the zoo. This is a real fear; let it ring loudly in your prefrontal cortex and guide you swiftly to safety.

Option B: Fear that is there to illuminate an uncertain path — a road not yet taken. Stay alert and aware of your surroundings by all means, but trust yourself to handle the situation. This is the fear you must overcome, the inner child scared of asking an adult for their ice cream. Hold it in your hand as an assurance that even though new can be scary, it doesn't make it bad. Calm your beating heart, and steady your shaky voice — tell fear, thank you, but I've got this — and then give it all you've bloody got.

A Note on Everything That Could Go Wrong

I can't speak for everyone else when I say this, but I have the unhelpful tendency to believe that examining the worst-case scenario of any given situation will protect me from it. It's a complex thing to think about, really, because, on the one hand, the contemplation does have the potential to make me realize that I'm just being silly and that there's not so much that could go wrong at the moment...

On the other hand — especially because of the way the world has felt infinitely more confusing, unpredictable, and exhausting the past couple of years, in particular — I'm left with the understanding that things, from time to time, really do have the potential to go horribly, horribly wrong.

Life is so incredibly precious, and tomorrow is never guaranteed.

People on all four corners of the earth are experiencing suffering and heartache in ways I am lucky enough to have never experienced. There are hate crimes, natural disasters, and media culture that seeks to divide people based on their preference for a presidential candidate, in a time when putting a plaster (band aid for my American friends) over a deeply flawed political system should matter least.

The point is that there are so many very real things in this life to be afraid of — but I don't want the fear of living to be one of them. In fact, if nothing else, this dire worst-case scenario way of thinking inspires and encourages me to face the things that scare me even more adventurously.

It's the notion that if everything *were* to completely go wrong, and if the world, as we knew it, was coming to an untimely end, I would know I didn't let it get the best of me —simply because that's exactly what facing your fears means.

I know that I don't want to hold myself back, even for a second, from the things that might one day bring me the most joy. I don't want to be afraid of talking to strangers, asking for ice cream, or failing so hard that I'm forced to dust myself off and remember why I took the leap of faith in the first place.

Because, when it really comes down to it, a life with a scoop of hard-earned vanilla ice cream is a whole lot sweeter than one without it.

If the worst *possible* thing to come from taking the risk is learning to live without the ice cream — certainly no worse off than before — then I think I can hack it.

I see you, I hear you, fear, and I'm choosing to ignore you because I'm not here on this planet to bow down to the fear of the unknown. The next step is just the process of accepting that there will indeed always be things to be afraid of. More often than not, however, fear is just an illuminating beam of light on all the things that lie just outside our comfort zones.

And comfort was never a very good excuse for anything.

Least of all, being unhappy.

Chapter 9 – 11 Behaviours that Happy People Refuse to Engage-in

As it turns out, it's not necessarily only the things happy people *do* that create their happiness, but also all the things they don't do. Happy people aren't just acting happy — they're also actively working to avoid the behaviours that screw up and steal from their happiness.

This is a list of eleven of those things. Avoid them wherever and whenever possible, and I guarantee that you'll be happier as a result.

Here's why.

1- Gossiping

In this case, gossiping doesn't merely mean sharing information about other people who may or may not be present at the time. Psychologically speaking, the practice of gossip stems from the desire to connect with someone based on a shared interest in the social status or circumstance of another.

At its core, gossiping can be used as a practical tool for navigating and upholding social norms — but there is a negative side to it, too.

"Often those that criticize others reveal what he himself lacks." ~ *Shannon L. Alder*

Anytime a general observation or social update creeps into 'talking badly behind someone's back' territory — especially if it involves the disclosure of private information — you can be sure never to find an authentically happy person on the sending or receiving end of the conversation.

This is simply because truly happy individuals don't see the point in devoting a single moment of their precious time to concerning themselves with the irrelevant going-ons of other people.

They don't tolerate it, and it doesn't interest them.

Happy people want others to be successful, stress-free, and, most importantly, just as happy as they are! Gossiping provides nothing but an unnecessary obstacle to this experience.

2- Berating (Themselves or Others)

Look, we already know that our brain chemistry can have a direct impact on the way we think and feel on a day-to-day basis (i.e. depression or bipolar disorder) *and* that the way we think and feel can also impact the physical chemistry of the brain.

What's more is that this occurs to *such* a great extent that we don't even have to hear the words come out of another person's mouth for it to deeply affect us. Simply by just contemplating the thought, or perhaps quickly commenting to ourselves out loud, is all it takes for our brains to notice. As my mother used to say, "don't call yourself stupid, or your brain will hear it and start to believe you... and then you'll really be in trouble."

"The happiness of your life depends upon the quality of your thoughts." ~ Marcus Aurelius

In this way, how a person speaks to themselves (or others) when no one else is around to hear reveals a substantial amount of information about their current relationship status with happiness.

Happy people understand that our thoughts do indeed shape our reality — hell, they *become* our reality.

Thus, nipping an unhelpful thought or judgement in the bud before it turns into a reality is the best way to proceed when it comes to the pursuit of happiness.

3- Toxic Positivity

That's not to say that there isn't a place for the healthy processing of negative emotions — to suggest otherwise would be doing everyone a massive disservice. Because, unlike berating someone or speaking resentfully towards oneself, not all negativity (when positively navigated) is, in fact, bad.

It shouldn't surprise you, then, that happy people don't waste their energy on trying never to be sad, angry, or upset. To do so would be to fall prey to a phenomenon referred to as 'toxic positivity,' one that stems from the fear of addressing uncomfortable feelings and emotions.

Toxic positivity can manifest in all sorts of different ways, from a well-intended but misguided "don't cry" or "well, it could be worse" statement to a more direct dismissal or denial of something being wrong.

Happy people understand that the experience of these very natural emotions is not in opposition to happiness; rather, it goes hand in hand with it. Being human is a packaged deal, and there's nothing to gain by ignoring the more difficult-to-deal-with aspects of life.

"You cannot protect yourself from sadness without protecting yourself from happiness." ~ Jonathan Safran Foer

Understand that happiness is found *in spite* of negative situations, circumstances, and sentiments — not in place of them.

Compromising their Values

"Happiness is when what you think, what you say, and what you do are in harmony." ~ Mahatma Gandhi

People who alter themselves and what they stand for in an attempt to cater to the ideals of others do so for a couple of reasons — none of which include because they are truly happy.

Whether it stems from a preoccupation with what others might be thinking, a fear of abandonment or rejection by a particular social group, or the sense of control gained via the act of people pleasing, making changes or compromises to one's core values only exacerbates the distance between that person and their happiness.

Conversely, people who are genuinely happy don't hesitate to make their happiness a priority *first*. They accept that not everyone has to agree with the way they do things and that it's not possible to see eye-to-eye on every given issue.

A big part of being happy results directly from being happy with oneself... which results directly from being authentically oneself. There is a time, and a place for compromise — your code of ethics, moral compass, and personal ethos is not it.

Worrying about Things they Can't Control

They say worrying about something is allowing yourself to suffer it twice, and on this particular point, I couldn't agree more. If the point of the things you can't control is that you can't, indeed, control them, then there's really not much else to do.

I'm not saying that by only exuding optimism, it's possible to manifest the perfectly happy life that we all, obviously, desire — but I am telling you that worrying about it won't ever increase your odds.

"True happiness is to enjoy the present, without anxious dependence upon the future." ~ Seneca

Much like happy people come to terms with their negative emotions as and when necessary, they tend to deal with their problems in much the same way: as and when (and only when) absolutely necessary.

This is because if a problem lies outside of a person's realm of control, then it's not necessary for them to act or react in any particular way at all. By definition, it is literally unnecessary. Happy people know this and redirect their mental energy accordingly.

4- Lying

Happy people do not often (or ever) lie. Why? Because they have confidence in their ability to navigate the ups and downs of life without dependence on insincerity or deceit.

"Happiness is not the absence of problems, it's the ability to deal with them." ~ Steve Maraboli

In this way, it makes no sense for a happy individual to habitually lie — to do so would be to add to their list of problems, not detract from it (I assure you, happy people do still have their problems).

What's more, is that lying has the unfortunate tendency to lead to more lying, creating a chain reaction of sorts that, one day, sooner or later bound to return and bite you in the ass.

Lying, as a behaviour, stems from trying to avoid the short-term discomfort of telling the truth — be it because of embarrassment, a perceived vulnerability, or a desire to control the situation at hand.

Happy people, however, know to place the truth into the category of things they cannot control and, therefore, should not waste their time worrying over.

5- Attaching Value to Expectations (especially of others)

In order for a person to get happy in the first place, they first have to get that they are the only one who has any degree of say in the matter. One of the ways a person can fail drastically at accomplishing this is by placing any expectations on external outcomes.

This is because when expectation turns to entitlement, a simple turn of events can feel like we're being robbed of something we thought was promised — while, in reality, we only have ourselves to blame.

Think of attaching value to expectations as handing someone (or something) the keys to the door that unlocks happiness for us. Chances are it's not really something you want to be giving away.

"Happy people are those who use a lower threshold in order to label an event positive." ~ *David Niven*

Happy people internalize the fact that happiness is not found in shiny objects or other human beings, and they account for this by maintaining low expectations. "Expect nothing and reward everything," as my father likes to say.

6- Attention-seeking

One of the fastest ways to tell whether a person is happy or not is to observe how much effort they put into trying to convince you they are.

You might be beginning to sense a trend here: happy people do not need nor seek validation, but a lot of unhappy people do.

"Actual happiness always looks pretty squalid in comparison with the overcompensations for misery."~ Aldous Huxley

Remember that attention-seeking doesn't necessarily have to manifest in boastfulness or try-hard behaviour — sometimes, it looks more like a series of poor decisions or a string of self-deprecating sarcasm.

Happy people are secure in their relationships and interactions with others and know that attention will be rightfully bestowed upon them where attention is due (and even if it isn't, they know they'll be okay)!

7- Complaining

Yes, happy people might very well just have less to complain about in general, and the possibility of this notion is far from lost on me, but — when it comes to the cause and effect of happiness — I'm willing to bet that the act of choosing not to complain about things actually plays a larger role in curating happiness than you might think.

This is because when we complain about something, we give it the attention that has to be pulled from somewhere else; attention that could be better spent on any range of positive acknowledgements in the form of appreciation, acceptance, respect, words of affirmation, reassurance, or paid compliments, for example.

Happy people comprehend that their attention is extremely limited, as well as definitively finite in nature. Every complaint, therefore, equals a missed opportunity to reframe an unfortunate situation (remember the Smiling Llama Science from earlier), which therefore equals a missed opportunity to practice being happy.

"If you aren't grateful for what you already have, what makes you think you would be happy with more."~ Roy T. Bennett

Try not to complain about what you don't have and try to think positively about everything that you do; there's a strong chance you'll leave feeling like you've gained something priceless.

8- Holding a Grudge

Forgiveness is not something we give to other people, but it is an olive branch we can extend to ourselves. Not only is holding a grudge a hell of a toxic way to spend one's free time, but it plays an active role in blocking the pathway to an individual's strivings for fulfilment.

Psychologically, grudges are nothing more than a matter of the ego — grudges are what occurs when a person feels victimized or wronged and decides that there's absolutely *no way* that they're not going to take it personally. In fact, it doesn't even occur to grudge-bearers not to take it personally…

"Cry. Forgive. Learn. Move on. Let your tears water the seeds of your future happiness."~ Steve Maraboli

Happy people, on the other hand, have become well-acquainted with the helpful practice of letting go.

People who choose the joy of happiness over the fleeting satisfaction of pettiness understand that nine times out of ten, it probably wasn't even personal. People — for the most part — have better things to do than deliberately bother you.

"Sometimes you can be happy, or you can be right." Another thing my father likes to say.

9- Regretting the Past

Finally, people who are happy certainly don't look to the past for reasons to be unhappy, just like they don't let their expectations of the future cloud their experience of happiness in the present.

"Don't waste your time in anger, regrets, worries, and grudges. Life is too short to be unhappy." ~ Roy T. Bennett

There can be a fine line between nostalgia and the positive rehashing of old memories and tales, and torturing oneself by repeatedly reliving a painful moment in time.

If there is happiness to be found — as any happy person would implore you to believe — it exists in the here and now and not the then and there. Regret is akin to worrying about the things you can't control with the added discomfort of the reminder that this was perhaps once a moment you *could.*

Happy people decide not to care about regretting the past. It's a shoulda,' woulda,' coulda' type situation, and we humans always tend to want what we can't have — in this case, that would be a redo.

And when it comes to being happy, I promise there's no merit to a rewind button or an undo. It's all part of the process. Learn to embrace it!

Chapter 10 – Choosing Your Hard to Improve Your Happy

Life is not lemonade; it's a series of under-ripe lemons being hurled at you at 45mph by an invisible machine, like the ones that launch tennis balls, but bigger and worse.

Life is not all fun and games — and if we're being real, it's not even like 35% fun and games. I do believe, however, that looking at life this way makes the other 65% of the pie of life just that *little* bit easier to cope with.

In truth, I think all aspects of life are a struggle (more on this in the next chapter). And ironically, I think accepting that fact makes me a happier, more optimistic human being.

You see, if we can come to terms with the difficulty setting of this game that we're all playing (it's set to level *hard*, by the way), then it becomes a whole lot less of a surprise when things go wrong in our life, or we feel insurmountably overwhelmed.

Put simply: Life is not easy — it's about choosing your hard.

Here's what that means exactly.

The Hards We Can't Control

There are troublesome areas of our lives that we simply have no choice over; these are the hards we can't control.

Because we can't control these hards, there is little point in me giving any type of advice on them. You are likely already doing your best to stay afloat and deal with the changing of the tides as and when they come.

The hards we can't control can be rough. The world we currently live in is not a very nice place to be for a lot of us, whether it's because of our skin colour, economic status, sexual preference, gender identity, or any of the other things that set us apart from what the media and society have falsely identified as the norm.

For the hards, we can't control — keep on doing what you're doing, fight the good fight, and know that there's a light at the end of the tunnel coming soon.

The Hards We Can Control

There are troublesome areas of our life that, as much as it might scare us to admit, we do have a choice in deciding. These are the hards we can control.

Eating healthy and sticking to a workout regime is hard; being unhealthy or overweight is also hard. Choose your hard.

Budgeting your money effectively and saying no to going out with friends is hard; being in debt and stressing about money is also hard. Choose your hard.

Learning to let go of things and move on is hard; holding a grudge and re-living past mistakes is also hard. Choose your hard.

Practicing honest communication in your interpersonal relationships is hard; communicating poorly and not having your needs met is also hard. Choose your hard.

Embracing change is hard; staying in the same place your whole life is also hard. Choose your hard.

Putting other people before yourself is hard; living selfishly is also hard. Choose your hard.

Loving yourself is hard; waking up every day and hating yourself is also hard. Choose your hard.

Bear in mind that none of these hards *aren't* hard — they all possess significant, if not equally challenging, degrees of difficulty and stress. They are part of a process that is designed, for the most part, to suck. It's called life.

Also, bear in mind that if, after a reflective and honest assessment, you find that a hard you thought you could control is actually a hard you can't control, then don't sweat it.

This is about making your life easier, after all, and about only spending your energy on the things you can change that will contribute positively to your long-term happiness.

If life is just suffering, then, at the very least, reap the benefits of choosing your hard.

Chapter 11 – The Joy of Philosophical Pessimism

A dear friend of mine... (Adam, if you're reading this, thank you kindly and genuinely for always playing devil's advocate in my life, and please do not ask me for a percentage of the royalties from this book; the answer is already no).

I digress.

A dear friend of mine has a theory — albeit not a very nice one — that my life is like a happiness pendulum and that although I may spend the first half of my life on a natural high, it will, inevitably, all come crashing down when the potential energy of my pendulum reaches its peak.

Despite my own personal determination to invalidate this theory of his, I came to realize it actually gave me more of a reason to be happy.

I mean — geez — if, in some twisted version of Newton's third law of motion, I'm doomed to one day face valleys equal but opposite in their depth to the height of my glorious peaks, then I might as well milk those happy highs for all they're worth.

Understandably, there was some feigned resentment when I shared this conclusion with him, but it got me thinking about how I engage with the topic of philosophy in general.

You see, for all intents and purposes, I fit the bill of a perfect optimist; I believe in human decency on an individual level, I lean towards positive psychology as a way to improve the life of myself and others, and — as I mentioned before — I'm pretty damn enthusiastic about being alive.

This is why it often surprises people when they learn I subscribe passionately to pessimism as a philosophy and that my all-time favourite historical figure is a blind poet born in 973 AD, Syria, who believed, in a nutshell, that all life is comprised of suffering.

I admit it sounds pretty dark, but I'd like to share why I think this way of thinking actually has the potential to brighten the way we experience this life (as heartbreaking and earth-shatteringly beautiful as it is).

"To live is to suffer; to survive is to find something worth suffering for."~ Friedrich Nietzsche

The Positivity of Suffering

Ancient philosopher, Al Ma'arri, was not a religious man. What I mean by this is that he did not suppose there existed a promise of salvation on behalf of a higher power, nor a heaven, nor a hell.

He believed the life we find ourselves with on earth is all we have.

What's more, is that Al Ma'arri concluded that, for the vast majority of human beings that will ever exist, their life would consist, for the most part, of a series of struggles, setbacks, and significant sufferings.

Most importantly, he believed that accepting this reality of life was the only sure way to overcome the pain associated with the delusion that the world is meant to be a wonderful place and to ease the sting of surprise when things do not turn out for the better for us.

There are no words that suffice to explain how much this mentality has helped me.

For as long as I can recall, I have been deeply affected by my perception of injustice. At age 8, I wept while watching King Kong, completely bereft that this animal was being hunted for its nature when man was the one trespassing on the island in the first place. At age 13, I sobbed for hours as the credits of The Imitation Game rolled on the screen; I couldn't fathom how a man who saved so many lives and contributed so enormously to the field of technology would be medically castrated and driven to take his own life by the unacceptance of his sexuality. At age 16, I went vegan, watching (through a blur of tears) slaughterhouse footage of the way we manufacture food out of living, breathing, sentient beings.

How completely unfair it all seemed.

There was a time when the suffering that existed in the world — visible to me from all angles — really messed with my faith in humanity, as well as my happiness, not to mention.

I distinctly remember being so angry, so incredibly frustrated that this was the way the dice had landed on the table as if, prior to my arrival, there had been some promise of peace and justice that was since reneged. I was gripped by the pain of the delusion that (I felt) had been sold to me, that the world was meant to be a wonderful place.

Pessimism, however, provided me with a new perspective.

Described as the tendency to believe that the worst, or, at the very least, something less than optimal, will happen, pessimism is a philosophy that sets our sights low and occasionally has the pleasant ability to surprise us when expectations are exceeded.

In other words, if we anticipate that life is full of suffering — both for ourselves and for those around us — then every passing moment that we're spared this horrendous fate will, inevitably, be perceived as a bonus. If a state of crisis is the accepted and understood norm, then moments of peace and neutral contentment can be observed with the same degree of awe we experience towards moments consisting of the spectacularly positive.

In a way, we are down-shifting the gears of our expectation in order to account for the very likely possibility that nothing will go our way — it's true, after all, that for a very large number of people born unto this life, it never does.

Poverty, pandemics, disease, and discrimination against disability. Sexism, racism, objectification, and endless exploitation. Car accidents, natural disasters, irreversible, un-take-back-able mistakes. The list of potential sufferings is never-ending, and, as any exterminator could tell you, the first step to eradicating the problem (sorry, bugs) is to first understand the extent of it.

Well, it just so happens that where human suffering is concerned, there is an extent. There is a huge extent, and there are problems neither of us will solve in our lifetimes nor those of our great-great-great-grandchildren.

In reality, there exists an overwhelming degree of injustice, with philosophical pessimism offering potentially the only source of freedom from the burden of believing that the natural state of things is a just and equitable one. I intentionally use the word *burden* here, for a reason.

Because it's vital to understand that it's not as though these ubiquitous instances of suffering went away the second I happened upon philosophical pessimism — or that I stopped experiencing empathy towards said sufferings to the same degree. Rather, by fully embracing pessimism, it meant merely that I was no longer burdened with the discomfort of feeling *cheated* by these facts.

"Voltaire once described optimism as 'a cruel philosophy with a consoling name,' which immediately suggests what pessimism might be: a consoling philosophy with a cruel name."~ Eugene Thacker

The Negativity of Happiness

I suppose if I were to stop writing at the end of the previous paragraph, I would be lending myself to the impression that I believe happiness arises exclusively from the absence of failed expectations and unfulfilled desires.

While it's fair to say that that's exactly what I believe, I feel it would be rude to leave things there without further explanation. I must add that this notion, as it pertains to the subject of happiness, is also by no means a new one.

Arthur Schopenhauer, a philosopher with beliefs not dissimilar to my beloved Al Ma'arri, was perhaps the first to point out that happiness is not quite what we think of it to be.

Schopenhauer once stated that happiness is "actually and essentially only ever *negative,* and absolutely never positive." But much akin to the mathematical concept of a double-negative, he claimed that happiness occurs via the satisfaction present in a negation of desire — meaning that happiness is what you get when the pain of wanting something is relieved.

He reiterates the idea that it's precisely where we hold an expectation for happiness to exist, that it will pass us by unobserved.

It's like how we only truly appreciate breathing from both our nostrils when a bout of the common cold reminds us that it's not a given, it's a privilege.

In this sense, if we feel as though health, happiness, or a general leaning towards good times is the baseline upon which we craft our desires, we are destined to fall short of happiness, time and time again. If happiness is the product of one's expectations divided by the sum of one's reality, then it seems to me that we ought to be expecting less in order to balance the equation.

Here, our own optimism has the potential to make us angry. We might feel as though we have been robbed of something that ought to have been guaranteed or that life has short-changed us when, realistically, we have been lucky to receive any gold coinage at all.

Antithetically, the adoption and implementation of a pessimistic mindset prepares us (in a positive way) for the worst and protects us from the shock of disappointment by placing the bar so unwaveringly low that life becomes unable to pull the rug out from underneath us entirely.

What once served as a reason for me to mourn the reduction of my own faith in humanity now becomes a platform upon which to marvel at any and all human efforts to be *good*.

If life is suffering, and hurt people hurt people, then the moments wherein a choice is made by an individual to rise above can be practically maintained as a miracle.

Neutral becomes positive, pain-free becomes perfection, and the occasional failure of reality to limit itself to the height of low expectations becomes a wonderful surprise appearance of that thing we refer to as happiness.

It's like expecting an empty glass and getting one only half empty...

SCORE!

Chapter 12 – It's Okay for Your Authenticity to Offend People

"I like offending people, because I think people who get offended should be offended." ~ Linus Torvalds

When you get pretty good at defending and protecting your own happiness, there's a very strong chance that, at some point, you'll contribute to someone else's experience of distinct *unhappiness*.

Just thinking about it, I'm certain I've pissed someone off before, probably just by walking into the room. I know for a fact that there are people that will find my decision to abstain from wearing a bra, occasionally but highly offensive (hello, growing up in ultra-conservative Alabama), and others that will judge me in a negative light for the way I talk, think, act, and behave — or not!

There are people I may upset with my occasional introversion and sometimes stand-offish demeanor, and I am equally confident that there will be times I get on the nerves of other people for almost the exact opposite reason… perhaps they'll say I talk too much, too loudly, and far too often. Maybe the way I'm writing this chapter will make someone angry.

Maybe they'll be offended just now that I've called them out.

So, while I've certainly (okay, mostly) never intended to rub anyone the wrong way, I have accepted that it's a fact of reality that we all must come to terms with.

A Fork in the Road to Authenticity

Despite all our best efforts to live an unproblematic life, there have been, no doubt — and there will very likely always continue to be — people who take offense to the choices and behaviours that characterize our happiness in life.

Whether it's our hair, our sexual preferences, or our existence, in general, we're damned if we do, and we're damned if we don't. Believe me when I say it's not possible to make yourself loved by everyone; hell, it's fairly difficult to even be liked by any significant majority — and at what cost exactly?

Let me put it to you this way:

Scenario A — You utterly commit yourself to authenticity and discover what it means to live your truth. The result will be that not everyone likes you this way.

Scenario B — You attempt to please others and shape yourself to fit the mold that society, your colleagues, your family, or society as a whole believes is best. The result will be that not everyone likes you this way.

The difference between these options is that, while both result in the inevitable reality that you will not be liked by everyone you come to encounter over the duration of your long life, at least the people in the first scenario don't like you for reasons that are actually based on *you*.

If you alter your own life preferences to accommodate the silly (and inevitable) offended people you interact with, then you risk adhering to someone else's truth entirely and spending your life wondering why you feel so lost and *un-you*.

You can't allow yourself to also join the bandwagon of individuals that dislike you, and when you compromise your authentic self, you open the door to an entire list of negative consequences like self-doubt, comparison, heightened insecurity, and over-criticality.

To be honest, I can't quite think of anything worse.

By giving a damn what other people do and do not concern themselves with when it comes to the choices you make in your personal life, you're allowing the people in the room to win before you've even had a chance to walk in and offend them with nothing but your existence.

Always go with scenario A and protect your happiness above the happiness of other people when it comes to living your truth — it's not selfish; it's self-care.

So What if I Offend You?

Tell me, what does offense *do* anyway?

I mean, I know exactly how it feels — it's abrasive and unpleasant and makes you wish you could control things that, in reality, it's much wiser for you not to. I know exactly how offense feels, but I never completely figured out what it does.

"It's now very common to hear people say, 'I'm rather offended by that.' As if that gives them certain rights. It's actually nothing more... than a whine. 'I find that offensive.' It has no meaning; it has no purpose; it has no reason to be respected as a phrase. 'I am offended by that.' Well, so f*cking what." ~ Stephen Fry

It's probable that you may find the above quote to be somewhat offensive, and please realize that the irony there is absolutely golden to me.

What Stephen Fry puts so very eloquently is that being offended is just that: being offended. There is no necessary action required to fight, overcome, or even prevent it from happening in the first place.

Being offended is a state of being, and there is an undeniable number of people who are committed to spending the majority of their existence in this state — no matter how trivial the subject of their taking of offense is.

We live in a time and place where there are plenty of things to be genuinely offended by. I'm not trying to suggest that offense has no purpose or that being offended by certain things is always a negative quality. I'm just here to remind you that someone taking offense to your tattoos, your disinterest in mainstream academia, or the way you prefer not to shave underneath your arms is not worth spending your emotional energy trying to address.

The Importance of Living Your Truth

What is your truth, exactly?

Well, it's anything that makes you feel like *you*. It's the wonderful and completely unique sum of all the things you like, the things you think, the things you do, the things you say, and the things you feel. It's your reality, your life, your truth.

So, stop trying not to offend people with your truth. It's yours, after all, and you should completely and absolutely own it.

If living your truth includes swearing a lot, not having children, never getting married, or dressing in a way that doesn't fit society's perfect little box of what a 60-something-year-old should wear, then you should commit to being okay with other people routinely taking offense to it.

Learn to view their disapproval, dismay, and the fact that they don't like you as a sign that you're on the right track, even.

By living your truth, you will begin to notice that the right people fall head over heels for you and that it's you admirably leading the way by example.

It's quite simply just not possible to make everyone else happy with your life, so you might as well live how you like and respond to the haters à la Stephen Fry by saying *so f*cking what?*

Just do what makes *you* happy.

Chapter 13 – The Simple Way to Guarantee a Life Without Regret

The only thing objectively worse than dying in this life is dying with regrets — and about this, I'm pretty sure.

Regret is an empty, numb feeling that sits in the pit of your stomach alongside the words you can never take back, the time you can never waste again, and the moments you can never relive.

The fear of regret, to me, is one hundred times more terrifying, more crippling than the fear of death or damnation. Regret is a curse of the human condition and one I wish to avoid at all costs. Regret is an emotion that will sabotage your current and future happiness and yell at you on its way out - HASHTAG NO RAGRETS.

Thankfully — and far less dramatically — I think I've figured out how to turn the tables on regret. And the answer is *effort*.

So the Brain Has a Thing for Effort

It's simple, really, when you understand it. Because while effort will never make promises to you, and it will never guarantee a specific outcome, effort will also never betray you.

Let me ask you a few questions to better illustrate my point:

Have you ever thought to yourself that you wish you had spent less time finger-painting as a child?

Or how about wishing that you never went to that really tough workout class last month?

What about regretting the time you spent 5 solid hours in a state of mental flow (that brain state where one's sense of time and space seems to entirely dissolve) while you typed up the first few chapters of the book you've always wanted to write?

No, no, and no, right?

This is because whenever we put effort into something (and it can be literally anything), we completely bypass the part of the wiring system of our brains that allows us to process and feel regret.

When individuals are experiencing a state of regret, the *ventral striatum* – an area in the prefrontal cortex of

112

the brain that is most associated with the processing of rewards and decision-making — will typically show a decrease in activity (26). Safe to say, we don't exactly find regret to be rewarding.

Meanwhile, the *amygdala* — a part of the brain's limbic system that creates a fight or flight response to various threats and stressors — will show an increase in brain activity (27). In this way, we find regret to be a very real threat to the adjacent areas of our life.

Interestingly enough, this reaction doesn't occur at all when individuals are absolved of personal accountability; witnessing someone else making a bad decision or seeing another person experience regret doesn't have nearly the same effect on our brains (thankfully).

In other words, in order for us to feel regret, there has to have been some degree of personal responsibility that we ignored, some conscious decision to do things a certain way that we now have to look back on with remorse.

While this may not exactly sound like good news, I promise you, it really is!

For starters, everyone knows that it's much easier to regret *not* doing something than it is to regret doing something. This is because we fundamentally understand that we, as human beings, are bound to make mistakes, but we can become much more critical of ourselves when it comes to letting opportunities pass us by.

While making mistakes might illustrate a short-term lapse in judgement, allowing factors such as a lack of self-confidence or the fear of rejection to hold us back might give way to deeper, more intrinsic flaws in the fabric of our character and identities.

In other words, it's some pretty scary stuff.

Alternatively, by mustering up the courage to put effort into something — whether it's learning a different language, launching a new business, or just finishing the rest of that book you put down three weeks (months?!) ago — we subsequently free ourselves from the potential to regret this action by taking away the personal accountability for the time spent engaging with it.

Now before you get too excited, let me remind you that effort does not make promises.

I'm not telling you that the road to success is paved with cobblestones that read, 'she worked hard, or 'he tried.' Sometimes putting in effort is the precise action it takes to realize that your dreams are just not attainable in their current condition.

Sometimes putting in effort will lead to a degree of failure that you've never experienced before — effort could end a career, a marriage, or both. Effort could reveal to you a whole lot about yourself that you never knew before, but I can guarantee you that effort will not leave you with any regrets.

So, write the book, set the goals, make the art, and risk the love.

Pour 110% of your effort into something that means *something*, and then repeat.

Repeat.

Repeat.

Repeat.

Repeat until you look back on your life and see nothing but time well spent, insights learned, and personal wisdom gained. Repeat until it becomes absolutely crystal clear that living a life without regret is just one less obstacle in your way of being happy.

After all, effort does not make promises, but effort will never betray you.

Chapter 14 – Eating Happy to Feel Happy

How and Why Plants Can Make You a Happier Person

Despite appearances (and popular stereotypes), I'm not actually hell-bent on making every last person I come into contact with aware of the fact that I'm vegan.

Rather, the subject of veganism itself acts as such an ongoing and positive source of inspiration for me that it would be unkind not to share my perspective. No, but really, the choice to trade in my SAD eating habits (a rather fitting acronym for the Standard American Diet) for a plant-based lifestyle centered around whole grains, legumes, and fresh fruits and vegetables, is quite simply one of the best decisions I've ever made.

Hand on my heart, it has ultimately improved *every* aspect of my life for the better.

Not only did going vegan serve as my initial prompt for getting up to speed on how to properly research and write about topics such as psychology, environmental science, institutionalized healthcare, and government policy (to name a few), but it also made me a more successful human being…

Success, in this context, is selfishly quantified by my own personal happiness. After all, I can't think of any better way to be successful than to be truly and abundantly happy, and I truly believe this whole *eating plants* thing has something to do with it.

As it turns out, I'm not the only one who feels this way.

A simple google search will return thousands of results about the benefits of a plant-based diet as they pertain to happiness — results that range from books and personal anecdotes to peer-reviewed research papers and everything in between.

So, here's my take on the whole thing — and I'm going to break it down for you, nice and simple: I think eating plant-based makes you happy in three key sectors of life. Namely, these are the physical, the mental, and the spiritual… and here's how.

Food that Nourishes the Body

"Flesh-eating by humans is unnecessary, irrational, anatomically unsound, unhealthy, unhygienic, uneconomic, unaesthetic, unkind and unethical. May I elaborate?"~ Helen Nearing

They say what you put in is what you get out, and there is an increasing number of studies that highlight the physical associations between a plant-based diet and benefits to mood, energy, and overall health.

In a series of recent experiments, it was found that individuals on a plant-based diet experienced significantly fewer negative emotions and reported an elevation in the mood more frequently when compared to their omnivorous counterparts (28).

Furthermore, the research found that people who eat predominantly plant-based are scientifically less likely to suffer from stress and the effects of anxiety — with meat-eating individuals who switch to a plant-based diet experiencing a noticeable reduction in stress levels after only two weeks (29).

If you're interested in the specific mechanisms of animal-based foods that scientists believe are responsible for their negative effects on well-being, rest assured, in the second section of this chapter, I've got your back.

First, consider for a moment the fact that 9 out of 10 of the top causes of death and disability in the U.S. are preventable, direct consequences of our eating habits — and ones that are proven to affect vegans significantly less. So, alongside the physiological improvements to well-being and general mood also exists the peace of mind that accompanies the state of simply *being healthier* (30, 31).

In addition to the obvious advantages to personal happiness that things such as living longer and avoiding many of the leading killer diseases might provide, people eating plant-based also suffer significantly lower rates of so-called "inconvenience ills;" these are things such as ulcers, migraines, hemorrhoids, varicose veins, minor surgeries, and frequent hospitalizations (of both major and minor kinds).

The plant-based community is also estimated to have around *half* the odds of needing pharmaceutical

drugs in order to function normally day-to-day —
including sleeping pills, laxatives, antacids, pain
medications, aspirin, insulin, and blood pressure
tablets (32).

It makes sense why a person avoiding all these
hassles might experience an elevation in mood.

What's more is that the consumption of higher
quantities of fruits and vegetables has unequivocally
been shown to result in levels of increased vigor,
calmness, and general happiness.

In fact, it's theorized that a higher consumption of
vegetables (somewhere around 6–10 servings per day)
may offer a decrease in the risk of developing
depression by up to 62% (33, 34).

If this is indeed the case — as the journal Nutritional
Neuroscience concludes — then switching to a plant-
based and/or vegan diet *can* and *should* be
considered a "non-invasive, natural and inexpensive
therapeutic means" of supporting a healthy and happy
brain (35).

This is exactly how I think eating plant-based can
make you a happier person *physically*.

Food that Nourishes the Mind

A peculiar thing happens when many people first go vegan, and that is they *feel* lighter.

Sure, this could just be the result of improved digestion or increased energy (both of which would fall into the section of the physical above), but I actually think it has more to do with a shift in mindset.

This is where we'll discuss a plant-based diet in the more specific context of veganism, AKA the "more-than-just-a-diet" state of eliminating harm to other sentient beings as far as the reality of our existence on earth permits. AKA not eating animals for ethical reasons — above all.

Research shows that, when asked, the vast majority of people will maintain that they love and, indeed, wish to protect animals from inhumane treatment. No doubt you would too.

But the fact is that the vast majority of people also choose to eat animal flesh, creating an automatic incongruence between their actions and beliefs that fits the definition of something referred to in psychology as cognitive dissonance (36).

This phenomenon — and specifically the *becoming free* of this mentally burdening phenomenon that coincides with the switch to a vegan diet — is what I believe contributes to this overwhelming feeling of a weight being lifted... of a lighter body and mind...when one goes vegan.

This is because when we experience cognitive dissonance, our vision of the world becomes clouded. We shift from a state of using our intellect to guide and craft our decisions throughout the day to one that focuses more on our perceptions, emotional responses, and ego.

I assure you, this is not just a matter of my opinion, but I do understand that this could be uncomfortable material to digest. (If it is, try referring to the takeaways from Chapter 7; where does this discomfort come from? Why is it there? And what's the worst thing that could happen should you choose to lean into it?)

To explore cognitive dissonance even further, experts in this field have found, time and time again, that people who have a greater tendency to perceive animals as inferior to humans also have a greater tendency to perceive other humans as inferior (37).

The reason for this is that as soon as we become comfortable with the mental inconsistency that arises when there's a difference between what we know (i.e. animal suffering is bad) and what we do (i.e. I like to eat animals), we also get better at applying this faulty logic to other areas of our lives (i.e. some humans are more superior than others).

With that being said — there is hope.

Research shows that the opposite is also true: individuals who have a greater tendency to perceive animals as similar to humans (i.e. we shouldn't be eating either of them) also have a greater tendency to express moral concern for our fellow humans (i.e. all animals, including humans, are equal and deserving of kindness). In the case of this particular research study, it was specifically moral concern towards immigrant and minority groups that was tested (38).

"When positive change has occurred, no matter how small, we feel the godliness within ourselves. As we see the goodness within ourselves, we recognize the good in others."~ Sandra Kimler

So, in terms of how eating a plant-based (vegan) diet can make you a happier person, it's not altogether improbable that happiness is really just the by-product of *being* a better person. A kinder, more understanding, empathetic, *morally-consistent* person.

I believe when you eliminate the incongruence between what comes out of your mouth and what goes into it, you are, in effect, allowing a more pure form of happiness to internally (and externally) advantage your life.

Food that Nourishes the Soul

What about the switch that occurs — not in physical health or subconscious perspective and mindset — but with regard to inner peace and energetic vibration?

Now, don't get me wrong, I take one look at the word vibration being used in an article, and more often than not (although less-so, nowadays), I click away. I'm all for people embracing whatever it is that floats their boat, but I like to keep both feet firmly on the ground when it comes to the discussion of scientific claims.

This, then, is the one section where I'm going to need you to just hear me out.

When I first went vegan, there were a handful of changes that I began to note. First and foremost, that sluggish post-meal-time slump was lifted and replaced with a mental refresh and an influx of energy. I stopped wanting to sleep immediately after eating my food and unlocked a wave of increased stamina instead.

My skin began to glow, the satisfaction of my new lifestyle practically spilling out of my pores. My self-confidence shot through the roof, and I ended the mental war I had waged against my body (and its reflection in the mirror) for the six to eight months of angsty teenage contemplation prior. I started tuning in to the needs of myself and those around me in a different, more acute way.

Along with a total refrain from the habit of criticizing myself also came the conscious provocation to stop judging others, too; the profound understanding that people can only meet you where they have met themselves was one that struck me particularly deeply.

My sensitivity towards violence, suffering, and aggression shot through the roof, and horror films and documentaries about crime no longer thrilled me — they drained me.

The plane of awareness upon which I functioned changed.

I leveled up.

I clocked on.

I shifted spiritually and emotionally for the better.

But is it really possible this all came as the result of a change in diet? Others, too, seem to think so.

"When you consume animal products, you ingest violence. You ingest the unimaginable fear and terror of the slaughterhouse. You ingest the profound, crushing sadness of a mother whose baby was taken away to be sold for veal. You ingest the distress of being crammed into a battery cage or "cage-free" prison until you are stuffed into a crate and killed in a most violent way. You ingest all of the suffering — and the death — of being who, like you wanted to live. There is mounting evidence that animal foods are detrimental to physical health. But I have no doubt at all that they are absolutely fatal to the health of the spirit."~
Gary L. Francione

You see, despite there being no way to scientifically measure the impact different foods may have on the health of the spirit, there are some things that just make sense.

Empiricism is the scientific method in its purest form, after all, and I know I speak for many vegans when I talk about how fulfilling it is to consume foods that never had to suffer to end up on my plate.

When you fill your stomach with foods that once had a heartbeat, with bodies that experienced one wave of adrenaline after another as they waited in a single file line for their turn with the bolt-gun, you become inevitably affected.

How could the reality be anything else? How could we eat death and suffering and expect to feel alive and happy?

Now, then, I am a firm believer that the less suffering you bring, the more compassion you feel, and the more compassion you feel, the more joy and love that you attract.

Most people I know would give an arm and a leg to feel this way, yet people are so quick to close their minds to any experiment involving veganism.

"The possibility of stepping into a higher plane is quite real for everyone. It requires no force or effort or sacrifice. It involves little more than changing our ideas about what is normal."~ Deepak Chopra

So this I have found to be inexplicably true. Eating plant-based does make you a happier person. Try for 6 months, maybe — perhaps you have nothing to lose, and everything to gain.

6 Foods That Might be Negatively Affecting Your Happiness (and Health)

Fascinatingly, my opinion above is backed by an increasing amount of research that suggests the pursuit of happiness might actually begin at our kitchen tables (aka with the food we eat).

This influx of recent findings is accompanied by major ramifications for the way we, as a culture, view the connection between food and mental health.

While it's been understood for decades that a diet centered around a large variety of different fruits and vegetables is associated with increased happiness, longevity, and overall well-being, it may be to our detriment that we never hear about the foods that may be actively detracting from our healthful efforts (39).

Here are some of the foods highlighted within the academic literature on happiness. And while I am a firm believer that knowledge is power, I certainly do not condone the use of the following list to support unhealthy eating restrictions surrounding food.

Take in the information, and then, in moderation, perhaps seek to implement it.

"The act of nutrition has been proven in research to have a direct correlation with the improvement of mental health." ~ Eva Selhub, MD from Harvard University

Sugary Drinks (Soda, Fruit Juice, Energy Drinks, Sweet Tea)

Unlike whole fruits, which naturally moderate insulin levels with the presence of fibre, fruit juice, and other sugary drinks, have been repeatedly linked to an increased risk of mood disorders, hyperactivity, and general depression (40).

Not only is a higher sugar intake linked to higher levels of unhappiness in general, but the immediate spike in blood sugar levels that accompanies these popular drinks means that your mood will likely take a hit even within the hour.

What's important to note is that research indicates that diet sodas and artificially sweetened drinks might actually be worse than their legitimate counterparts. Aspartame, for example — the controversial sweetener used in thousands of drinks, dressings, and desserts — has been routinely associated with the experience of sadness and irritability of mood, due to its potential modulation of certain neurotransmitters, such as dopamine and serotonin, within the brain (41).

Refined Carbohydrates (White Bread, White Flour, White Pasta, Pastries, Cakes, Cookies, Processed Cereals)

Ladies and gentlemen, it's no coincidence that researchers and nutritionists alike have nicknamed the Modern American Diet and the Standard American Diet MAD and SAD, respectively. And due to the Western diet's unhealthy focus on sugars, refined carbohydrates, and high trans-fat containing foods, it's no wonder that in areas where this lifestyle of eating is most heavily adhered to, the prevalence of mood disorders and depression continues to rise.

Meals rich in processed foods and refined grains cause exaggerated spikes in sugar and fat within the body, leading to the generation of free radicals.

Free radicals are the molecules responsible for mutations within the body that can wreak havoc on lipids, proteins, and DNA, raising the likelihood of disease in the process. The oxidative stress that results from these biochemical food reactions subsequently triggers our brain to enter a mild form of fight-or-flight mode, dramatically increasing our experience of anxiety and unease (42).

Poultry (Chicken, Turkey, Goose)

There is a compound called tryptophan which is an amino acid and one of the building blocks of serotonin. Studies have shown that people with deficiencies of this compound suffer from irritability, anger, and often depression as a result (43).

What's more, is that while complete serotonin does not possess the ability to cross between the blood-brain barrier, tryptophan does. This would lead us to believe that consuming animal foods highest in tryptophan — such as chicken and turkey — would be beneficial... right?

Wrong, I'm afraid.

The problem is that animal sources of tryptophan are also high in other amino acids, which crowd the brain for entry, thereby blocking tryptophan out.

Plant-based foods, however, trigger a release of insulin that helps your muscles uptake non-tryptophan amino acids as a source of fuel, giving your brain clear access to the tryptophan it needs. In fact, a direct comparison study found that a carb-rich breakfast such as whole-grain waffles and fruit resulted in higher (initial and maintained) levels of tryptophan in the brain, versus a breakfast comprised of protein-rich foods such as turkey, eggs, and cheese (44).

Alcohol (Whiskey, Wine, Beer, Tequila, Liqueurs)

Regardless of the mood we're in when we take that first sip, both low and high levels of alcohol consumption have been shown to be related to an increased risk of experiencing negative emotions or, rather, a decreased ability to regulate distress or sadness.

For some, drinking can even be linked to aggression, with epidemiological studies suggesting that the effects of alcohol consumption may lead to a decrease in intellectual reasoning within the prefrontal cortex of the brain that, when coupled with perceived provocation, may result in elevated levels of anger, anxiety, and anti-social behaviour (45).

Indeed, we can probably all vouch for the fact that if alcohol really isn't putting a damper on our happiness while we're drinking it, the subsequent hangover to follow the next morning certainly might.

Seed Oils (Soybean Oil, Canola Oil, Sunflower Oil, Sesame Oil)

Hydrogenated oils such as soybean and sesame oil are comprised of up to 60% of a compound known as Omega-6 (also known as linoleic acid). Despite the healthy-sounding nature of this term, there can be disastrous effects that arise from having too much of it in your system.

In fact, research demonstrates that there is a significant correlation between the ratio of Omega-6 to Omega-3 and poor mood health (46). This is because both types of fatty acids compete with one another, and there's a strong tendency for an excess of one to knock the other one completely out.

In the last century, our consumption of soybean oil, alongside other seed oils, has risen by 56,000%. Make sure to check out the ingredient labels on processed foods, too, as companies love to use seed oils in their products due to their relative inexpensiveness.

Interestingly, it's not actually the Omega-6 in the seed oil itself that causes issues, rather, it's what occurs when linoleic acid gets converted to arachidonic acid within the body. This acid has been significantly linked with an adverse impact on mental health via a cascade of inflammation that occurs in the brain upon ingestion, with data suggesting that higher levels of arachidonic acid are related to a higher risk of suicide and major depressive episodes (47).

Eggs

The trouble with arachidonic acid is that although we do require small amounts of it for our bodies to successfully fight off disease and infection, we already produce 100% of what we will ever need — meaning that any extra taken in via our diet will have some degree of negative consequences.

While the only plant sources of arachidonic acid include algae, mosses, and ferns — substances unlikely to be consumed in quantity or on any regular basis — all animal products are found to contain the chemical, with the five highest sources being chicken, eggs, beef, pork, and fish.

Note that eggs, in particular, contain more arachidonic acid than all the above sources combined, with research indicating that even eating as little as a single egg per day was enough to significantly raise the levels of inflammation within the brain (48).

Overall, omnivores were found to consume about nine times more arachidonic acid than their plant-based counterparts, providing some additional context for the benefits of a diet centered around whole foods, fruits, and vegetables and the well-documented advantages to happiness it holds!

Thank you for coming to my TED talk (I do promise to shut up about veganism now) and for holding the space for me to discuss a less-than-always-palateable (pun intended) subject with you.

Chapter 15 – 12 Ways to Make Your Day Almost Instantly Better

"Tell me, what is it you plan to do with your one wild and precious life?" ~ *Mary Oliver*

Well, since you asked, Mary Oliver — and seeing as it is the final chapter of this book — I'll tell you. I'll tell you that I'd like to live a life of truly magnificent adventure. A novel-worthy expedition with excitement, romance, and inspiration at every turn and one that sets my heart aglow with the sheer joy of what it means to be human.

In the meantime, however — and in the in-between time — I think I'd just like to be happy.

Recently, I've become acutely aware of how easy it is to get caught up on the major plot points of life: the promotions, the proposals, the grand gestures, and the even grander celebrations.

Yes, indeed, I don't think I speak only for myself when I say destination addiction is a real affliction that all too often results in a tendency to overlook the smaller, day-to-day opportunities to be happier and more fulfilled. In an effort to balance this propensity to look ahead to one's future with longing eyes and a wishful mind, I have made a conscious effort, as of late, to create little pockets of happiness for myself — small actions that boost overall positivity, and ones, that when turned to habit, can significantly impact overall life satisfaction.

I leave you and Mary Oliver with this one last list, as I present 12 ways to make your day (almost) instantly better. I hope you'll happily take them with you as you go (and bonus points if you can identify which neurotransmitters these activities might be triggering in the brain)!

Practice Makes Happy (Not Perfect)

Drink a Glass of Water

Go on...go and get that glass of water — down the hatch it goes. If we're going to be doing this the right way, then it's paramount that we start off with proper hydration. The rest of the book will still be here when you return.

It's nothing you haven't heard before, but drinking water helps combat fatigue, electrolyte imbalance, headaches, as well as a bad mood or frame of mind. Give yourself the best chance of having a great day by kicking up your water intake by a few notches. Cheers to that!

Express Gratitude Tangibly

Science (aforementioned in Chapter 6) suggests that it's impossible to simultaneously experience anxiety and gratitude. In other words, when our brains consciously process and choose to focus on the things we're grateful for, our stressors subsequently become minimized in their capacity to control us.

It becomes very hard to wallow in self-pity or spend time worrying about things out of our control when we take time to reflect on how lucky we are to have the life we do.

In order to ramp up the positive effects gratitude can have on your present mood/day/life, take a moment to express it tangibly (i.e., in a way you can look back on) to another person.

Text your friend, call your mother, thank your boss, bake something for your neighbor (or show up with some beer if that's more your style)! Always be grateful for the things you have, and you'll forget to think twice about the things you don't.

Stretch or Move Your Body

I was watching a Ted Talk the other day that emphasized the importance of 'getting into' your body each and every day. The notion that we must wiggle our toes, bend our bodies, and stretch our legs once a day seemed to resonate with me.

All too often, we spend time in our heads, going about our day in a 'think-y' state of interaction and reaction. As peculiar as it may sound, reminding ourselves that our bodies come with physical features — and ones that require being moved and exercised *often* — boasts a wealth of benefits pertaining both to an immediate happiness boost due to the release of endorphins, as well as increased life satisfaction in the long-term.

Walk, run, skip, dance, climb, reach, bend, stretch, MOVE!

Eat a Piece of Ripe, Brightly Coloured, Juicy Fruit

More often than not, the colour of fruits and vegetables directly relates to the level of antioxidants they contain.

This means when faced with deciding between a red and green apple, or a white or purple onion, perhaps, — preference and particular recipe requirements aside — you should opt for the more colourful of the two (the red apple, and purple onion, that is).

Further to this, research shows that individuals who consume more fruit daily not only experience a lower risk of disease and mortality in the long-term, but also experience an increase in life satisfaction, happiness, and overall well-being, as far more of an immediate side-effect than one might think (49).

There's a reason mother nature created one of the healthiest foods on the planet to exist in a range of vibrant hues, from blood orange to beet red, with the added characteristic of tasting sweet. So, find some fruit you know you like, or better yet, try a new one and thank me later.

Make a List of 5 Things You're Proud of Yourself for

There might be dozens of hopes you have for the future and a million things on your to-do list, but it's vital to take the time to appreciate how far you've already come.

We all have a tendency, from time to time, to be far too harsh on ourselves, failing, in the process, to acknowledge that life itself can be rather tough. Jot down a quick 5-item list of the things you can be proud of yourself for, and reflect on the feeling of accomplishment and contentment.

Here's mine (and it's important you include the 'I'm proud' part):

I'm proud of myself for learning how to cook a greater variety of nutritious meals this year.

I'm proud of myself for having the balls to put my writing out there in the form of this e-book (yikes!).

I'm proud of myself for letting certain relationships, apartments, and unhelpful mindsets go.

I'm proud of myself for working as hard and as purposefully as I do.

I'm proud of myself for being able to see the bigger picture when dealing with a difference of opinion among certain family members. (You know who you are, haha)!

Your turn!

Sit in the Sunshine, or Go for a Walk

Not only does sitting in the sunshine feel good to our body, it also encourages mood elevation and re-energization inside (and brains) by increasing the levels of the neurotransmitter serotonin. Individuals with higher levels of serotonin are shown to experience better moods day-to-day, a lower risk of anxiety and depression, as well as general feelings of calmness and joy.

Research examining the effects of sun exposure on serotonin levels found that no matter how hot or cold the weather was, people had higher levels of serotonin flowing out of their brains on sunny days versus cloudy ones.

By taking a 15-minute walk outside or sitting your butt down on a sunny patch of grass, you'll not only be increasing your serotonin levels but also ensuring you get enough vitamin D — a nutrient that also plays a major role in mood regulation.

Revisit Something that Makes You Really Laugh

This could mean re-reading a chapter in a favourite book, watching a YouTube video, listening to a segment of stand-up on the radio, or even just re-hashing an embarrassing moment with an old friend.

142

You don't have to get uber-creative or think far outside the box to find a little piece of happiness in your day. In fact, relying on the tried and trusted methods of lifting your mood will feel just as good as it did the first time. We have favourites for a reason, people — don't forget it!

You know you best, so go forth and find something to make you giggle.

Compliment a Stranger (or Ten)

Now, if the idea of having to compliment complete strangers perturbs you, then you can always start out by complimenting a colleague, family member, or close friend.

The trick is to pay attention to yourself when you notice something you like about them. Are they wearing something particularly eye-catching today? Did you find something they said earlier really insightful or hilarious? Maybe even both.

Make a point of mentally appreciating them, and then go one step further in sharing it verbally — it matters far less what it is you choose to compliment these strangers on and far more that you took a moment to gift these people with a happy dose of words of affirmation.

I'm a firm believer that what goes around comes around, and you should never underestimate the positive power of brightening someone else's day: an instant dose of happiness or your money back — guaranteed!

Plan Something Fun and Out of the Ordinary

Having something — anything — to look forward to in the near future will immediately provide a sense of satisfaction and excitement for what's to come. This could be as simple as scheduling some time before a busy workday to enjoy a drink at the fancy tea place you always wanted to try or maybe deciding to re-arrange and re-decorate the living room.

It could also mean something more thrilling, like planning a spontaneous trip to New Orleans with your best friend (because why not? — life is short) or committing to going speed-dating once a month to expand your social circle or to get better at conversing with strangers.

Maybe that all sounds like a nightmare to you, but the point is: plan something that gets your heart beating that little bit faster and relish the anticipation of looking forward to it.

Listen to a Song that Always Makes You Want to Dance

It might just be me who feels this way, though I sincerely hope not. I'm talking about those songs you listen to — whether walking down the street or driving — that are just so damn *punchy* and energetic that you can't help but want to dance, skip, or sing.

Well, I'm giving you permission (not that you asked for it) to fully embrace the ridiculousness of dancing in a public space and to feel completely amazing while doing so! Trust me when I say that anyone watching will only be envious of your joy — they'll want exactly what you're having and more.

Some current personal favourites to publicly embarrass myself include:

- 'Comeback Kid' by Brett Dennen
- 'Electric Feel' by MGMT
- 'Rock and Roll Never Forgets' by Bob Seger & The Silver Bullet Band
- 'To Noise Making' by Hozier
- 'Double Negative' by Dominic Fike.

Sit Consciously for X-amount of Minutes

Now, I personally go through phases with meditation — or perhaps I just refer to it as something else — but there is definitely something to be said for taking the time to consciously reflect on the present moment.

Sit somewhere cozy, or have a lay down, and cherish the feelings of happiness and personal fulfilment that arise. Take yourself somewhere peaceful mentally and do this until you get bored. Nothing magical will happen (at least it doesn't for me), but I find that I never regret the time I spend having a moment to myself, away from the treacherous grasp of technology and media, just to think about things.

Introspection is a powerful tool, and there is no doubt it helps to foster happiness when used correctly.

Make a Checklist and Complete It

Copy and paste these 12 items into your notes app and check them off as you go. The physical act of organizing your accomplishments in this visually satisfying way will lend itself to an immediate sense of gratification.

1. Drink a glass of water

2. Express gratitude tangibly

3. Stretch or move your body

4. Eat a piece of fruit

5. Make a list of 5 things you're proud of yourself for

6. Sit in the sunshine, or go for a walk

7. Revisit something that makes you really laugh

8. Compliment a stranger

9. Plan something fun and out of the ordinary

10. Listen to a song that always makes you want to dance

11. Sit consciously for x amount of minutes

12. Complete the checklist

Feel any happier? Me too.

Acknowledgements

Thank you, first and foremost, to David Harper at Amazon Publishing Pros for walking me through the start-to-finish process of self-publishing a book and for being honest enough to tell me that some of my questions were *a little odd.* If it weren't for your Author's Questionnaire, I would likely not have an acknowledgements page to be thanking anyone on.

Thank you to my parents, to whom I have dedicated this book, for always encouraging me as a writer, even amidst my protest that that was not what I ever wanted to be. You have often known me better than I have known myself, and I feel extraordinarily grateful to have had the honour of being raised by you. I will cry if I go on, so that's enough about you, I'm afraid.

Thank you to my siblings, Ethan, and Isabel, for the healthy competition—and for kindly pointing out that I wouldn't stand a chance should I instead choose to pursue a professional career in sports. Thank you to Doon-Doon for putting up with my workaholic tendencies and supplying endless cups of tea, more often than not, with an outrageous story to accompany. No one believes me when I say that my 89-year-old, 4ft, 10in grandmother was once on the front cover of the local newspaper for starting a fistfight, but that is another book for another day! A very special thank you to Gramps. I have no doubt that my fondness for writing is a much-loved hand-me-down from you. Thank you to my partner Louis for keeping life exciting and light, for making it your unspoken mission to make me laugh each morning, often before I even realise I'm awake, and for choosing to love me for exactly me. I am so very grateful that you exist.

Lastly, thank you, you — whoever you are — for reading my book. I hope it was what you expected, and if not, then at the very least, a pleasant surprise.

There are a great many other thank you's I wish to name, but I shall take it upon myself to do those personally and save making this short little book on happiness too long.

About the Author

Alexandra is a research and creative writer, published author, and communications manager currently living in Surrey, England.

Her early interests in psychology, nutrition, and the science of health & wellbeing have inspired her to publish over 200 articles online, as well as complete a 1st class honours degree in Psychology and Sociology from Regent's University London.

She currently works for sofi.health, a startup in the world of wellness technology and plant-based medicine, and, in her spare time, as one of the founding team members of Prodolce, the one-of-a-kind, vegan-certified sparkling wine (available at www.prodolce.com).

References

1.   Dfarhud, D., Malmir, M., & Khanahmadi, M.
(2014). Happiness & Health: The Biological Factors-
Systematic Review Article. Iranian journal of public
health, 43(11), 1468–1477.

2.   Grippo RM, Purohit AM, Zhang Q, Zweifel LS,
Güler AD. Direct Midbrain Dopamine Input to the
Suprachiasmatic Nucleus Accelerates Circadian
Entrainment. Curr Biol. 2017 Aug 21;27(16):2465-
2475.e3.

3.   Evrensel, A., & Ceylan, M. E. (2015). The Gut-
Brain Axis: The Missing Link in Depression. Clinical
psychopharmacology and neuroscience: the official
scientific journal of the Korean College of
Neuropsychopharmacology, 13(3), 239–244.

4.   Mitchell RL, Phillips LH. The psychological,
neurochemical and functional neuroanatomical
mediators of the effects of positive and negative mood

on executive functions. Neuropsychologia. 2007 Mar 2;45(4):617–29.

5.   Carter CS. Neuroendocrine perspectives on social attachment and love. Psychoneuroendocrinology. 1998 Nov;23(8):779–818.

6.   Diener E, Seligman ME. Very happy people. Psychol Sci. 2002 Jan;13(1):81–4.

7.   Dfarhud, D., Malmir, M., & Khanahmadi, M. (2014). Happiness & Health: The Biological Factors-Systematic Review Article. Iranian journal of public health, 43(11), 1468–1477.

8.   Rokade PB (2011), Release of Endomorphin Hormone and Its Effects on Our Body and Moods: A Review International Conference on Chemical, Biological and Environment Sciences (ICCEBS)Bangkok.

9.   Boyd Eaton, S. (2010). Complex Chronic Diseases in Evolutionary Perspective. In M. Muehlenbein (Ed.), Human Evolutionary Biology (pp. 491–501). Cambridge: Cambridge University Press.

10.   Chakravarthy MV, Booth FW. Eating, exercise, and "thrifty" genotypes: connecting the dots toward

an evolutionary understanding of modern chronic diseases. J Appl Physiol (1985). 2004 Jan;96(1):3–10.

11. Allen, N. B., & Badcock, P. B. (2006). Darwinian models of depression: A review of evolutionary accounts of mood and mood disorders. Progress in Neuro-Psychopharmacology and Biological Psychiatry, 30(5), 815–826.

12. Hidaka B. H. (2012). Depression as a disease of modernity: explanations for increasing prevalence. Journal of affective disorders, 140(3), 205–214.

13. Schieffelin, E. L. (1985). The cultural analysis of depressive affect: An example from New Guinea. Culture and depression, 101–133.

14. Wakefield, J. C. (2007). The concept of mental disorder: diagnostic implications of the harmful dysfunction analysis. World Psychiatry, 6(3), 149.

15. Kendell, R. E. (1986). What are mental disorders? In A. M. Freedman, R. Brotman, I. Silverman, & D. Hutson (Eds.), Issues in psychiatric classification: Science, practice and social policy (p. 23 – 45). Human Sciences Press.

16. Kim, E. J., Pellman, B., & Kim, J. J. (2015). Stress effects on the hippocampus: a critical review.

Learning & memory (Cold Spring Harbor, N.Y.), 22(9), 411–416.

17.   Hölzel, B. K., Carmody, J., Vangel, M., Congleton, C., Yerramsetti, S. M., Gard, T., & Lazar, S. W. (2011). Mindfulness practice leads to increases in regional brain gray matter density. Psychiatry research, 191(1), 36–43.

18.   Grant, A. M., Franklin, J., & Langford, P. (2002). The Self-Reflection and Insight Scale: A new measure of private self-consciousness. Social Behavior and Personality: An international journal, 30(8), 821–836

19.   Janowsky, D.S. Introversion and extroversion: Implications for depression and suicidality. Curr Psychiatry Rep 3, 444–450 (2001).

20.   Marion, S. B., & Thorley, C. (2016). A Meta-Analytic Review Of Collaborative Inhibition And Post-Collaborative Memory: Testing The Predictions Of The Retrieval Strategy Disruption Hypothesis. Psychological Bulletin, 142(11), 1141–1164.

21.   Nance, W. Z., & Mays, M. (2013). Exploring The Role Of Time Alone In Modern Culture. In American Coun-Seling Association Conference, Cincinnati, Oh.

22.   Jeffrey A Hall, Andy J Merolla, Connecting Everyday Talk And Time Alone To Global Well-Being, Human Communication Research, Volume 46, Issue 1, January 2020, Pages 86–111.

23.   Knapp, C. E., & Smith, T. E. (2005). Exploring The Power Of Solo, Silence, And Solitude. Association For Experiential Education. 3775 Iris Ave., Suite 4, Boulder, Co 80304.

24.   de Voogd, L. D., Kanen, J. W., Neville, D. A., Roelofs, K., Fernández, G., & Hermans, E. J. (2018). Eye-Movement Intervention Enhances Extinction via Amygdala Deactivation. *The Journal of neuroscience : the official journal of the Society for Neuroscience, 38*(40), 8694–8706.

25.   Salay, L.D., Ishiko, N. & Huberman, A.D. A midline thalamic circuit determines reactions to visual threat. *Nature* 557, 183–189 (2018).

26.   Nicolle A, Bach DR, Driver J, Dolan RJ. A role for the striatum in regret-related choice repetition. J Cogn Neurosci. 2011 Apr;23(4):845-56.

27.   Nicolle, A., Bach, D. R., Frith, C., & Dolan, R. J. (2011). Amygdala involvement in self-blame regret. Social Neuroscience, 6(2), 178-189.

28.   Beezhold BL, Johnston CS. Restriction of meat, fish, and poultry in omnivores improves mood: a pilot randomized controlled trial. Nutr J. 2012 Feb 14;11:9

29.   Beezhold B, Radnitz C, Rinne A, DiMatteo J. Vegans report less stress and anxiety than omnivores. Nutr Neurosci. 2015 Oct;18(7):289–96

30.   Murray CJ, Atkinson C, Bhalla K, Birbeck G, Burstein R, Chou D, Dellavalle R, Danaei G, Ezzati M, Fahimi A, Flaxman D, Foreman, Gabriel S, Gakidou E, Kassebaum N, Khatibzadeh S, Lim S, Lipshultz SE, London S, Lopez, MacIntyre MF, Mokdad AH, Moran A, Moran AE, Mozaffarian D, Murphy T, Naghavi M, Pope C, Roberts T, Salomon J, Schwebel DC, Shahraz S, Sleet DA, Murray, Abraham J, Ali MK, Atkinson C, Bartels DH, Bhalla K, Birbeck G, Burstein R, Chen H, Criqui MH, Dahodwala, Jarlais, Ding EL, Dorsey ER, Ebel BE, Ezzati M, Fahami, Flaxman S, Flaxman AD, Gonzalez-Medina D, Grant B, Hagan H, Hoffman H, Kassebaum N, Khatibzadeh S, Leasher JL, Lin J, Lipshultz SE, Lozano R, Lu Y, Mallinger L, McDermott MM, Micha R, Miller TR, Mokdad AA, Mokdad AH, Mozaffarian D, Naghavi M, Narayan KM, Omer SB, Pelizzari PM, Phillips D, Ranganathan

D, Rivara FP, Roberts T, Sampson U, Sanman E, Sapkota A, Schwebel DC, Sharaz S, Shivakoti R, Singh GM, Singh D, Tavakkoli M, Towbin JA, Wilkinson JD, Zabetian A, Murray, Abraham J, Ali MK, Alvardo M, Atkinson C, Baddour LM, Benjamin EJ, Bhalla K, Birbeck G, Bolliger I, Burstein R, Carnahan E, Chou D, Chugh SS, Cohen A, Colson KE, Cooper LT, Couser W, Criqui MH, Dabhadkar KC, Dellavalle RP, Jarlais, Dicker D, Dorsey ER, Duber H, Ebel BE, Engell RE, Ezzati M, Felson DT, Finucane MM, Flaxman S, Flaxman AD, Fleming T, Foreman, Forouzanfar MH, Freedman G, Freeman MK, Gakidou E, Gillum RF, Gonzalez-Medina D, Gosselin R, Gutierrez HR, Hagan H, Havmoeller R, Hoffman H, Jacobsen KH, James SL, Jasrasaria R, Jayarman S, Johns N, Kassebaum N, Khatibzadeh S, Lan Q, Leasher JL, Lim S, Lipshultz SE, London S, Lopez, Lozano R, Lu Y, Mallinger L, Meltzer M, Mensah GA, Michaud C, Miller TR, Mock C, Moffitt TE, Mokdad AA, Mokdad AH, Moran A, Naghavi M, Narayan KM, Nelson RG, Olives C, Omer SB, Ortblad K, Ostro B, Pelizzari PM, Phillips D, Raju M, Razavi H, Ritz B, Roberts T, Sacco RL, Salomon J, Sampson U, Schwebel DC, Shahraz S, Shibuya K, Silberberg D, Singh JA, Steenland K,

158

Taylor JA, Thurston GD, Vavilala MS, Vos T, Wagner GR, Weinstock MA, Weisskopf MG, Wulf S, Murray; U.S. Burden of Disease Collaborators. The state of US health, 1990–2010: burden of diseases, injuries, and risk factors. JAMA. 2013 Aug 14;310(6):591–608.

31.   Lenders C, Gorman K, Milch H, Decker A, Harvey N, Stanfield L, Lim-Miller A, Salge-Blake J, Judd L, Levine S. A novel nutrition medicine education model: the Boston University experience. Adv Nutr. 2013 Jan 1;4(1):1–7.

32.   Knutsen SF. Lifestyle and the use of health services. Am J Clin Nutr. 1994;59(5 Suppl):1171S–1175S.

33.   White BA, Horwath CC, Connor TS. Many apples a day keep the blues away-dialy experiences of negative and positive affect and food consumption in young adults. Br J Health Psychol. 2013;18(4):782–98.

34.   Tsai AC, Change T-L, Chi S-H. Frequent consumption of vegetables predicts lower risk of depression in older Taiwanese- results of a prospective population-based study. Public Health Nutr.2012;15(6):1087–92.

35.   Gomez-Pinilla F, Nguyen TTJ. Natural mood foods: the actions of polyphenols against psychiatric

and cognitive disorders. Nutr Neurosci. 2012;15(3):127–33.

36.   Bastian B, Loughnan S. Resolving the Meat-Paradox: A Motivational Account of Morally Troublesome Behavior and Its Maintenance. Pers Soc Psychol Rev. 2017 Aug;21(3):278–299

37.   Bastian, B., Costello, K., Loughnan, S., & Hodson, G. (2012). When closing the human–animal divide expands moral concern: The importance of framing. Social Psychological and Personality Science, 3(4), 421–429.

38.   Costello, K., & Hodson, G. (2010). Exploring the roots of dehumanization: The role of animal — human similarity in promoting immigrant humanization. Group Processes & Intergroup Relations, 13(1), 3–22.

39.   Evrensel, A., & Ceylan, M. E. (2015). The Gut-Brain Axis: The Missing Link in Depression. Clinical psychopharmacology and neuroscience : the official scientific journal of the Korean College of Neuropsychopharmacology, 13(3), 239–244.

40.   Lien, L., Lien, N., Heyerdahl, S., Thoresen, M., & Bjertness, E. (2006). Consumption of soft drinks and hyperactivity, mental distress, and conduct problems

among adolescents in Oslo, Norway. American journal of public health, 96(10), 1815–1820.

41.   Lindseth, G. N., Coolahan, S. E., Petros, T. V., & Lindseth, P. D. (2014). Neurobehavioral effects of aspartame consumption. Research in nursing & health, 37(3), 185–193.

42.   Asmat U, Abad K, Ismail K. Diabetes mellitus and oxidative stress-A concise review. Saudi Pharm J. 2016 Sep;24(5):547-553

43.   Wurtman JJ, Brzezinski A, Wurtman RJ, Laferrere B. Effect of nutrient intake on premenstrual depression. Am J Obstet Gynecol. 1989 Nov;161(5):1228–34.

44.   Wurtman, R. J., Wurtman, J. J., Regan, M. M., McDermott, J. M., Tsay, R. H., & Breu, J. J. (2003). Effects of normal meals rich in carbohydrates or proteins on plasma tryptophan and tyrosine ratios. The American journal of clinical nutrition, 77(1), 128–132.

45.   Moeller, F. G., & Dougherty, D. M. (2001). Antisocial personality disorder, alcohol, and aggression. Alcohol research & health : the journal of the National Institute on Alcohol Abuse and Alcoholism, 25(1), 5–11.

46. Kiecolt-Glaser, Janice K. PhD; Belury, Martha A. PhD; Porter, Kyle MAS; Beversdorf, David Q. MD; Lemeshow, Stanley PhD; Glaser, Ronald PhDDepressive Symptoms, omega-6:omega-3 Fatty Acids, and Inflammation in Older Adults, Psychosomatic Medicine: April 2007 — Volume 69 — Issue 3 — p 217–224

47. Vaz, J. S., Kac, G., Nardi, A. E., & Hibbeln, J. R. (2014). Omega-6 fatty acids and greater likelihood of suicide risk and major depression in early pregnancy. Journal of affective disorders, 152, 76–82.

48. Adams PB, Lawson S, Sanigorski A, Sinclair AJ. Arachidonic acid to eicosapentaenoic acid ratio in blood correlates positively with clinical symptoms of depression. Lipids. 1996 Mar;31 Suppl:S157–61.

49. The Global Burden of Disease Study 2010 (GBD 2010)

Printed in Great Britain
by Amazon

22074136R00096